09

One Man Out

LANDMARK LAW CASES

&

AMERICAN SOCIETY

Peter Charles Hoffer
N. E. H. Hull
Series Editors

For a complete list of titles in the series go to www.kansaspress.ku.edu

ROBERT M. GOLDMAN

One Man Out

Curt Flood versus Baseball

UNIVERSITY PRESS OF KANSAS

Tim Peeler, "Curt Flood," in *Touching All the Bases: Poems from Baseball* (Jefferson, N.C.: McFarland, 2000), used by permission of the author.

Published by the University Press of Kansas (Lawrence, Kansas 66045), which was organized by the Kansas Board of Regents and is operated and funded by Emporia State University, Fort Hays State University, Kansas State University, Pittsburg State University, the University of Kansas, and Wichita State University

Library of Congress Cataloging-in-Publication Data

Goldman, Robert Michael.
One man out : Curt Flood versus baseball / Robert M. Goldman.
p. cm. — (Landmark law cases & American society)
Includes bibliographical references and index.
ISBN 978-0-7006-1602-2 (cloth : alk. paper)
ISBN 978-0-7006-1603-9 (pbk. : alk. paper)
1. Flood, Curt, 1938–1997—Trials, litigation, etc. 2. Antitrust law—United States.
3. Baseball—Law and legislation—United States. 4. Discrimination in sports—United States—Biography. 5. African American baseball players—Biography. I. Title.
KF228.F57G65 2008
344.73'099—dc22
2008016874

British Library Cataloguing-in-Publication Data is available.

Printed in the United States of America

10 9 8 7 6 5 4 3 2 1

The paper used in this publication is recycled and contains 30 percent postconsumer waste. It is acid free and meets the minimum requirements of the American National Standard for Permanence of Paper for Printed Library Materials Z39.48-1992.

In memory of Milt, Ruth, and Arn — my original team

CONTENTS

American lawsuits are all about the adversarial process. There are winners and losers. In that sense, they are just like baseball games. While a game may be postponed or replayed, no game ends in a tie. Winners take all. Losers go home and comfort themselves with "wait till next year." The winners of pennants and world series stand as landmarks in our sports landscape. The losers are rarely remembered (except for old Brooklyn Dodger fans, who can recall every loss to that other team from the Bronx).

Can a lost lawsuit then ever be a landmark? Robert Goldman's deeply moving and swiftly paced study of Curt Flood's suit against the owners of the St. Louis Cardinals and organized baseball's reserve clause proves what can be won by playing the game, even if one loses in the end. For the reserve clause was a kind of indentured servitude that Congress and the courts allowed long after other forms of bound labor had been abolished. The reserve clause made players into the property of their teams, to be bought and sold like any other commodity.

St. Louis Cardinal outfielder Curt Flood, an all-star player, would have none of this. A man of deep feelings and strong convictions, he had suffered through racial discrimination; annealed by its fires, he rejected the trade that his owners made sending him to another team. While money was a part of the matter, the real issue was personal autonomy, or perhaps even more precisely, what made a man into a man.

Perhaps the courts were the wrong place to try this question, for long before they had decided that baseball, the national pastime, was exempt from the antitrust statutes barring monopoly in other enterprises (including professional sports leagues). In the end, Flood lost his suit, but the players' union negotiated "free agency" with the owners' association, and free agency now dictates who plays for whom. Flood did not benefit from this sea change, and perhaps his suit did not cause free agency, but it did dramatize the plight of the players and ultimately made free agency seem natural.

Goldman tells the inside story of the case, revealing Flood's complexities along with the complexities of sports law, and he does it all in highly readable fashion. Goldman follows Flood's life after the suit, a denouement that is both uplifting and sad. Perhaps it is too strong a comparison to link Flood to Rosa Parks, whose refusal to change her seat in a Birmingham, Alabama, segregated bus was the opening round of the modern Civil Rights movement. Parks will never be forgotten, and Goldman's book will insure that Flood's story is remembered.

PREFACE

In the 1949 hit comedy movie *It Happens Every Spring*, the actor Ray Milland portrayed an eager but underpaid college chemistry teacher and former ballplayer who accidentally discovers a substance that repels wood. In love with the college president's daughter but too poor to ask for her hand in marriage, he joins a hapless professional baseball club (St. Louis, ironically) as a pitcher. Thanks to the secret substance, hidden in his hair tonic, he becomes unbeatable as opposing batters swing wildly at his pitches, missing a ball that refuses to make contact with their wooden bats. Of course the team goes from last place in the league to win the World Series. But, alas, on the last play of the Series the hero hurts his hand and is told he can no longer pitch. As he waits to board the train back to his university to try to regain his job and his girl (both successfully, since this is, after all, Hollywood), he explains to his team roommate and best friend: "A lot of things make no sense. . . . I was a chemistry teacher . . . and the sum of money I received for teaching science to the youth of this state was a little less than I got in a single afternoon throwing a five-ounce sphere at a young man with a wooden stick."

The movie, especially that bit of dialogue, has always had a special resonance for me, and perhaps others like me who represent a particular cohort of Americans. I refer to academics of the baby-boom generation who grew up in an era when baseball seemed truly the "national pastime" and who believed, as the baseball writer Thomas Boswell put it, that "time begins on opening day." I also imagine that there are a fair number of college professors who, like me, have at one time or another taught or advised a student athlete who managed to make it to the professional level of his sport, where he earned far more than either we or Ray Milland's movie character could ever have imagined. I know I taught, and reluctantly twice failed, one such future star. I once calculated that at the height of his career, he made more just getting *dressed* for a single game than I did in a year! I also had a student who graduated at the top of his class, went on to law school, and is now beginning to make his mark, and a good living, not as an athlete but as an *agent* for professional athletes. That both these men are living their different versions of sports and the "American dream" is a matter of constant amazement to me, tinged no doubt with a bit of jealousy—just like that movie character.

I am also of a generation of American males for whom baseball in particular was not just the "national pastime"; it was *our* pastime, and our passion. Several years ago the legal historian and baseball maven Paul Finkelman sent me a copy of his marvelous essay "Baseball and the Rule of Law." In it he wrote of the "convergences" of the "culture of baseball" and the "culture of law" in American society. It was a revelation of sorts because it put together elements of my own background that I had never consciously thought about before. I grew up in Chicago in the 1950s and 1960s, and baseball provided me with some of my best and worst memories. I learned the game's fundamentals from Hall of Famer Luke Appling, whose declining years were spent, courtesy of Mayor Daley's (the elder) patronage largesse, traveling around Chicago's public parks in the summer to teach young boys like me the joys of the game. It was also Appling who wisely predicted that I should not plan on any sort of career in baseball. Like so many young men of that era, I was introduced to the world of big league baseball, especially the Chicago White Sox and Comiskey Park, by my father. He was an attorney who had worked his way through junior college and DePaul University College of Law by selling scorecards and hot dogs at Comiskey Park, and sometimes at the Cubs' Wrigley Field. As a young man I spent summer afternoons in his law office filling in the supplemental pages to *Corpus Juris Secundum* and nights with him at the ballpark, usually watching the Sox lose (except for the miracle year of 1959, when they were actually in the World Series). Despite this background, I must admit to having no specific personal recollection of Curt Flood and his lawsuit. Those years encompassed my hiatus from baseball. I was in graduate school and more concerned with my draft status and future employment prospects than with baseball. My only baseball connection then came from reading Roger Angell's graceful, elegant essays in the *New Yorker*. Yet at some point I managed my own reconvergence between baseball and the law. I have been teaching constitutional and legal history for almost thirty-five years, and every summer for the past decade my Thursday nights have been spent playing softball with my fellow baby boomers in the Chesterfield County Senior Softball Association (my first team, like Curt Flood's, was the Cardinals).

I mention all this not simply to explain why I wanted to write this book, and why I've enjoyed writing it, but also as a disclaimer of sorts about the intent of this volume. This book is most certainly not a history of baseball, a topic that I've discovered comes complete with entire libraries, journals, and professional organizations such as the Society for American Baseball Research (SABR). There are many folk, both inside and outside academia, who are devotedly committed to telling the story of this game in all its remarkable detail and variety. Neither is the book a history of African Americans in sports, for that too has most gratifyingly been the subject of serious and intensive historical study in recent years. Lastly, this volume does not pretend to be a full and complete biography of Curt Flood. In the past few years at least three such studies have appeared, all prodigiously researched and each with its own perspective on the life, character, and career of this remarkable individual.

This book, rather, tells the story of that man, baseball player Curt Flood, and his lawsuit against baseball following his refusal, after twelve stellar years with the Cardinals, to be traded from St. Louis to Philadelphia. It attempts to explain his case in both its legal and historical perspective and setting. Because of what was called the reserve system, Flood was by no means the first player in baseball history to be traded, nor even the first African American major leaguer to be so treated. From organized baseball's earliest years, players were bought, sold, and traded regularly. In 1957, Jackie Robinson, the first African American to play major league baseball, was informed that after ten brilliant years with the Brooklyn Dodgers, he was being traded to the Dodgers' crosstown National League rival, the New York Giants. Having received a lucrative offer to work for the Chock Full o'Nuts coffee company, Robinson chose to simply retire from baseball altogether. During the 1950s, Robinson was one of the few players who did speak out against the reserve clause and one of the few players who testified on Flood's behalf during his trial. Nor was Curt Flood the first baseball player to seek resolution of his complaints through our legal system. Going back to the days of Monte Ward and Nap Lajoie and the beginnings of organized baseball, there is a history of players, as well as club owners, settling their grievances and disputes in a court of law.

During his lifetime and after his death, Curt Flood was described in many different ways. He has been called a hero, a martyr, a leader, a pioneer, a visionary, a role model, a victim, a fraud, and even a revolutionary. He was variously characterized as talented, graceful, serious, sensitive, proud, humble, intelligent, articulate, and selfless. Others labeled him greedy, ungrateful, angry, gullible, manipulative, haughty, dishonest, and even cowardly. Being African American, he was also described in words and ways that are not worthy of repeating. Although his actions and his cause seemed straightforward and unambiguous, he often appeared much less so. Alex Belth, one of Flood's recent biographers, was probably correct when he confessed that there are aspects of Flood's life and personality that will never really be known or understood. One of those ambiguities involves race. Curt Flood was not just a ballplayer, he was an African American ballplayer who grew up and experienced life and professional baseball during years of revolutionary racial upheaval and change in American society. Curt Flood was young enough to have experienced firsthand the tragedy and outrage that was racial segregation, both the legal kind and the Oakland, California, de facto kind. He was old enough to live and play baseball during an era that witnessed the movement that successfully challenged at least the legal kind of racial discrimination. But he was also sensitive and wise enough to understand that things such as racism and prejudice don't go away. Flood would later write, "I am pleased that God made my skin black. I just wish he had made it thicker." Perhaps the greatest irony in this regard occurred when Flood described himself as a "well-paid slave." Because he was challenging a system that affected all players, black and white, his self-reference, though honest and historically resonant, was largely irrelevant to the legal issues in the case as it progressed through the courts. One of the claims first made in Flood's lawsuit was that baseball's reserve system was a violation of the Thirteenth Amendment, which had abolished slavery in 1865. The claim was summarily rejected by both the District Court and the Court of Appeals and was not even brought up in the final appeal to the Supreme Court. Only in Justice Thurgood Marshall's dissenting opinion in the case was there any reference to the idea of servitude. But Marshall, the first African American on the Court, applied it to all players, not just Flood. He conceded that for "non-athletes" it might have looked as if Flood were "virtually enslaved" to the owners. But "athletes know it was not servitude that bound petitioner [Flood] to the club owners, it was the reserve system."

Yet as Professor Gerald Early has shown, race played a role in how the press and public (Marshall's "non-athletes"?) reacted to the case. Not surprisingly, the black press was "generally sympathetic and supportive" of Flood's actions and saw his refusal to be traded and subsequent lawsuit as a "heroic" act of defiance against the "white-dominated system." It was Flood's critics who used the "well-paid" part of Flood's claim in an insidious way. For these critics, Flood's actions were a form of "ingratitude." In the "mythology" of slavery, he was like those slaves who were treated "well" by paternalistic masters and who were expected to show their gratitude by unquestioning obedience. But long after Flood's challenge of professional baseball's "plantation mentality," as Early concluded, he still "would be more the darling of the white left than he would ever be of the black civil rights establishment or of black-nationalist minded thinkers."

Given the fact that Flood ultimately lost his suit, it may be a fair question to ask what makes this case significant and worthy of "landmark" status. Even Supreme Court Justice Harry Blackmun, who wrote the majority opinion in *Flood v. Kuhn*, confessed that "in some respects the case wasn't very important." On the other hand, Justice Blackmun had no doubt that it was his "favorite" case and the one he had the most "fun" writing. He pointed out that when he spoke before various groups, especially young people, a mention of the Flood case caused their eyes to "light up" — they recognized instantly what he was talking about because it was the "baseball case." The legal antitrust and labor policy issues involved in the case were hardly front-page news, but the fact that the case involved the "national pastime," and a player as well known as Curt Flood, made it a matter of national interest and discussion. And even though Flood lost, there is little doubt that, as historian Charles P. Korr concluded, "his sincerity and determination went a long way to convince the players that there was a battle worth fighting."

Baseball is a game of numbers. The statistics, or "stats," as they're sometimes called, are religiously used to determine the performance and significance of everyone and nearly everything connected to baseball. *Flood v. Kuhn* has some impressive legal "stats" of its own. According to the most recent count, it has been cited in more than 800 law cases, 509 law-review articles, 5 congressional statutes, and 20 treatises. The Supreme Court's opinion is reprinted in sports-law and labor-law casebooks, and several years ago Flood appeared in an edited volume titled *100 Americans Making Constitutional History*. He has also been the subject of a number of film documentaries as well as two recent book-length studies. As I write, professional sports, especially baseball, is in the midst of its own "perfect storm," with scandals and investigations regularly making the nightly news. The public seems to have grown cynical and sadly accustomed to hearing and reading about athletes and the law in terms of congressional and grand-jury inquiries, indictments, and criminal defense attorneys. In his recent book, *Dropping the Ball*, Hall of Fame outfielder Dave Winfield catalogs "baseball's troubles and how we can and must solve them." Baseball's problems are not limited to the use of performance-enhancing drugs by the players. As an African American, Winfield is especially concerned with what he calls the "new color line" in baseball and the "plummeting" numbers of African American players — and fans. He cites the fact that in 1975, 28 percent of major leaguers were black. By 2006, that number had dropped to 8 percent. By itself, telling the story of a remarkable ballplayer like Curt Flood is not nearly the whole solution to any of these problems. But perhaps it is a step in restoring some of the optimism and amazement displayed by the characters in that 1949 movie. At the very least, the story of this case is a reminder of the unique and important place that baseball and the law have in American society.

The writing of history is not generally thought of as a "team" effort like baseball. Rather, the image tends to be that of the lone historian working amid piles of notes and books at his or her desk, or in some dusty archive or library, researching, thinking, and writing in solitude. To me, this image is a bit dated, and it certainly doesn't square with the writing of this book. Libraries and piles of notes have been replaced by computers and the Web, and the Internet has allowed for near-instantaneous contact with colleagues and sources in ways unimaginable to previous generations of scholars. I therefore feel both obliged and honored to acknowledge my "teammates" in this endeavor. Of course ultimate responsibility for what is said or not said in the following pages is mine alone.

First, there are those historians and scholars whose own efforts to examine various aspects of baseball's story have helped me enormously.

Although they receive credit in the bibliographical essay, a number of them have been especially important in shaping my understanding of baseball's past and its convergences with the law. They include Charles B. Korr, Paul Finkelman, G. Edward White, Robert F. Burk, Roger I. Abrams, Jerrold Duquette, and Alex Belth. I also want to thank Jay Topkis, one of Flood's trial attorneys. He graciously answered questions about the case and some of the individuals involved. I concur with Marvin Miller's assessment that had Topkis and not Goldberg handled the case through the Supreme Court, the outcome might have been different. Tony Freyer, Mel Urofsky, Neil Lanctot, and Ken Wasserman were among a number of people who also answered questions or clarified certain points, sometimes trivial ones, about baseball and constitutional history. Professor Roger I. Abrams provided a careful and helpful reading of my manuscript. I also want to express my appreciation to the editors of the Landmark Law Cases & American Society Series, N. E. H. Hull and Peter Hoffer, for their patience and support. I am especially indebted to Michael Briggs, editor-in-chief at the University Press of Kansas, and his wonderful staff at the press. Even though Mike is a Cubs fan, I'd play for his team any day. As promised, I also want to thank my niece Jami Goldman. Her computer expertise and navigational skills with Lexis-Nexis and Westlaw have rescued me on more than one occasion. She is currently a law student, and I am confident that one day she will be the first in our family to actually argue a case before the Supreme Court.

I also want to express my appreciation to the "roster" of friends, family, and colleagues whose support and encouragement has been invaluable. They include my Chicago family, aunts and cousins, and my family by marriage, including Terry, Nancy, Jeff, Leslie, David, Regan, and a future baseball prospect, Drew. Thanks as well to Les and Karen Benedict, Jim Johnson, Eileen Wagner, and Alan and Phyllis Entin. I would also like to mention my fellow baby boomers in the Chesterfield County Senior Softball Association, especially Artie, Ray, Ike, and Ruby. I hope they enjoy this book as much as I've enjoyed playing ball with them over the years. Finally, I want to thank my wonderful stepdaughter, Sue, who showed up to help at just the right moment, and my wife, best friend, and all-star utility player, Sandie. As always, Sandie helped me get through the tough innings, even as she was going through some pretty tough ones of her own.

The First Inning

The summer and early fall of 1969 had proven to be a long, frustrating season for the St. Louis Cardinals, especially for their twelve-year veteran and all-star center fielder, Curt Flood. Over the past decade, his team had played in three World Series, winning two of them in 1964 and 1967. This year, with an expanded National League divided into Eastern and Western divisions, the Cardinals had finished fourth out of six teams, thirteen games behind the surprising New York Mets. Flood could take little solace in his own record on the diamond. His season's batting average of .285 was respectable, but changes made in baseball in 1969 to make the game more conducive to hitters, such as expanding the strike zone and lowering the pitchers' mound, did not even place Flood in the top fifty hitters. It was especially frustrating because the previous year Flood's .301 average and 186 hits had placed him fifth in those two categories.

There was more to his situation than was revealed by the usual baseball statistics. As an African American, Curt Flood had been especially sensitive to what he termed the club's "social achievements." He had praised the 1967 and 1968 teams as being as "free of racist poison as a diverse group of twentieth-century Americans could possibly be." According to Flood, the players—blacks, whites, Latinos, and "redeemed peckerwoods"—truly "cared about each other and shared with each other." That camaraderie seemed absent during the 1969 season. Moreover, Flood's relationship with the team's management had changed for the worse. Gussie Busch was the president of the Anheuser-Busch Brewing Company, the company that owned the Cardinals franchise. Until the 1969 season, Busch had been a stalwart supporter of Flood, and, at least in Busch's mind, something of a surrogate father figure. But during spring training, Flood had been injured in a game with the New York Mets. The injury required stitches and a shot that resulted in Flood oversleeping and missing the team's promotional banquet for season-ticket holders. "No offense is less forgivable than that," Flood recalled. For his "thoughtless failure to awaken in time," he was fined $250. He protested "angrily," but to no avail. For the rest of the season, he would continue to speak out, realizing that each time "was another nail in my coffin. I was not speaking well of my boss. At $90,000 a year, I no longer looked so good in a hotel lobby. My days were numbered." Flood would further antagonize management when, during the regular season, he and several other veteran players questioned Cardinals manager Red Schoendienst's decision to place two rookie players in the team's batting order in positions that would cause opposing pitchers to "pitch around" better-proven hitters such as Flood and fellow outfielder Lou Brock. Although Schoendienst would relent and restore the Cardinals' previous lineup, Flood was convinced that the manager had been directed by the higher-ups in the organization to make the change in the first place because of their displeasure with Flood.

With the season finally over, a tired, frustrated Flood prepared to leave his home in St. Louis for a much-anticipated visit to Copenhagen, Denmark. On October 8, three days before his departure, he received a call from Jim Toomey, the assistant to the Cardinals general manager, Bing Devine. Flood himself remembered their brief conversation:

"Hello, Curt?"
"Yes.
"Jim Toomey, Curt."
A chill entered my belly. . . .
"Curt, you've been traded to Philadelphia."
Silence.
"You, McCarver, Hoerner and Byron Browne. For Richie Allen, Cookie Rojas and Jerry Johnson."
Silence
"Good luck, Curt."
"Thanks. Thanks a lot."

The following day Flood received a one-sentence letter on the team's letterhead from the general manager indicating that his contract had been assigned "OUTRIGHT" to the Philadelphia Club of the

National League. Also enclosed was baseball's version of a "pink slip," an index-card-sized standardized form, "Notice to Player of Release or Transfer." The form was numbered "No. 614," with Flood's name written in and the option lines signifying that the player had been released crossed out. Curt Flood had been traded, not fired, so the choice was simple. "I can go to Philadelphia or I can quit baseball altogether. I will not go to Philadelphia." After informing Devine of his decision to retire from baseball, Flood left for Europe.

Upon his return, Flood met with Phillies general manager John Quinn, who happened to be in St. Louis. At this meeting, Quinn tried to convince Flood to play for the Phillies by painting an optimistic picture of the future of Philadelphia and its baseball club. Now uncertain about what to do, Flood contacted a local St. Louis attorney, Allan H. Zerman. Zerman had helped Flood set up his photography business and had also assisted his brother Carl. Zerman, Flood recalled, "was the only man who had ever refused to take World Series tickets from me." And although Flood had thought about it before, it is likely that the attorney was the first to suggest to the center fielder that he sue baseball.

Flood then contacted Marvin Miller, the head of the Baseball Players Association, who invited Flood and his attorney to a day-long series of meetings in New York City. As Miller remembers the talks, he told the two men that the case "had merit" but that "we would lose because they [the baseball owners] protect their rear ends." Miller explained about court precedents that had ruled against the players and for the reserve clause. He warned Flood that if he were to bring a lawsuit, it would likely take two to three years and "cost a fortune." It might also mean the end not only of his playing career but of any future involvement with baseball. "When I say these people are vindictive, I mean I would not put it past them to end any possibility you might have — I don't know what your feeling is about being a coach or manager — but realistically you'll have to forget that too." Miller also intimated that the owners would be inclined to find and use any unsavory details about Flood's personal life. Although Flood was ready to go forward with a lawsuit, Miller recommended that he return to St. Louis and think about it. To complicate things further, Flood also met with the Phillies' Quinn, who raised the team's salary offer to $100,000.

Flood returned to St. Louis and, as Miller had advised, "holed up" in his apartment and considered his next move. He realized that he lacked the fortune that Miller had indicated would be necessary to carry through a legal battle, but "I was fortified by what I am not ashamed to call spiritual resources."

"Marvin, I'm going ahead with it. Can you help?" To get the support of the Baseball Players Association, Flood would need the approval of the association's executive board, made up of player representatives from each of the Major League franchises. As it happened, the board was about to hold its winter meeting in San Juan, Puerto Rico, and since time was of the essence if anything was to be done before the start of the next baseball season, Flood flew down to San Juan to personally plead his case before the board. Tim McCarver, Flood's teammate and the Cardinals' player representative at the time, met Flood in Miami on their way to Puerto Rico. McCarver recalls: "That's when I found out firsthand how serious he was about doing this thing, and that's when it first started sinking in that this was indeed a very big move he was making."

On December 13, 1969, Flood met with the board and spoke for about an hour and a half. According to his own account, and those of Miller and McCarver, Flood provided the players with a clear and sincere explanation of his opposition to the reserve clause as well as a totally honest appraisal of the "negatives" that a legal challenge to the system entailed. After he finished speaking, Miller "encouraged the guys to go ahead and ask anything they wanted to. And Curt answered everything in a straightforward fashion." The most obvious question was what exactly Flood wanted from the association by way of "assistance." He told them that if his lawsuit was to have any chance of success, he would need a "top-notch antitrust attorney," and since he could not afford one, he wanted the association to pay the attorneys' fees and any expenses he would incur as a witness in the case. He also agreed that even if the owners offered him a lot of money to drop the suit, he would not do so. Any damages he might be awarded should he be victorious would be given to the association.

In the course of the questioning, one of the players, Tom Haller, a catcher with the Los Angeles Dodgers, raised an issue that the others had been reluctant to bring up. Haller asked Flood if he was doing this because of his race and as a victim of racial discrimination. Again

Flood responded forthrightly, admitting that "I'd be lying if I told you that as a black man in baseball I hadn't gone through worse times than my white team-mates." And he recognized that at that moment in time, there was a heightened consciousness of racial prejudice in America. But he emphasized that what he was doing was ultimately as "a ball-player, a major league ball-player"; he felt that for too long the players had put up with this "situation" and not stood together to resist it. Now, Flood stated, was the time to do something.

After Flood left, the board voted "unanimously" to support his law-suit, although as it transpired, not all players in the association agreed with that decision. One player, Carl "Yaz" Yastrzemski, the all-star slugger with the Boston Red Sox, sent an angry letter to Miller complaining that the reserve clause was such an important issue to the players and the association that all of them should have been consulted beforehand. Yastrzemski pointed to a questionnaire that had been sent to all the players the previous year regarding a possible players' strike over pension issues. Although he wrote that he was not taking a position on the "merits" of the case, in an interview with reporter Will McDonough of the *Sporting News*, Yastrzemski had openly expressed his dismay over players' "constantly taking" from the owners. Yaz, who happened to be one of the highest-paid players at the time, felt that challenging the reserve clause by legal action might well create a "gap" between owners and players that "couldn't be repaired."

As promised, when Marvin Miller returned from Puerto Rico he contacted his first choice for an attorney to represent Flood. Arthur Goldberg, then in private practice in New York City, was a former Supreme Court justice and U.S. representative to the United Nations. Miller's relationship with Goldberg stretched back more than twenty years to the time when both men had worked for the United Steel-workers union, Miller as a labor analyst and negotiator and Goldberg as a labor-law specialist. Based on his personal experience, Miller had an extremely high regard for Goldberg's advocacy talents, and after explaining the Flood case to the ex-justice was delighted by Goldberg's positive response. Two issues had to be addressed first, however. At the time of their meeting, reports were circulating that the Democrats in New York were interested in getting Goldberg to run for governor against the incumbent Republican Nelson Rockefeller in the November 1970 election. Miller was concerned that a political campaign would leave Goldberg little time for handling a case that, with a trial and appeals, could take a year or more. According to Miller's account of their meeting, Goldberg assured him that he had no interest in running for governor, and "since it didn't seem possible that we could get a better lawyer than Arthur Goldberg, I decided to trust him." The other issue that needed to be worked out was compensation. Although the Baseball Players Association had agreed to foot the bill for the case, the association had limited financial resources, and Goldberg would not come cheap. Goldberg, however, indicated that he would do the case pro bono, except for "expenses, travel, and whatnot"—although he did ask that associates from his law firm be paid for any hours they spent on the case. Miller was delighted. "This was much better than anything I had hoped for. Arthur Goldberg for expenses! That was like Sandy Koufax pitching for pass-the-hat."

With Goldberg and his team on board, it was time for Miller and the association to help Flood "fire the first shot." On December 24, 1969, Christmas Eve, Curt Flood sent the following letter to Commissioner of Baseball Bowie Kuhn:

Dear Mr. Kuhn:
   After 12 years in the major leagues, I do not feel that I am a piece of property to be bought and sold irrespective of my wishes. I believe that any system that produces that result violates my basic rights as a citizen and is inconsistent with the laws of the United States and the several states.
   It is my desire to play baseball in 1970 and I am capable of playing. I have received a contract from the Philadelphia club, but I believe I have the right to consider offers from other clubs before making any decisions. I, therefore, request that you make known to all the major league clubs my feelings in this matter, and advise them of my availability for the 1970 season.

Six days later Kuhn replied:

Dear Curt,
   This will acknowledge your letter of December 24, which I found on returning to my office yesterday.
   I certainly agree with you that you, as a human being, are not a

{ *Chapter 1* }

piece of property to be bought and sold. This is fundamental in our society and I think obvious. However, I cannot see its applicability to the situation at hand.

You have entered into a current playing contract with the St. Louis club, which has the same assignment provision as those in your annual major league contracts since 1956. Your present contract has been assigned in accordance with its provisions by the St. Louis club to the Philadelphia club. The provisions of the playing contract have been negotiated over the years between the clubs and the players, most recently when the present basic agreement was negotiated two years ago between the clubs and the Players Association.

If you had specific objection to the propriety of the assignment, I would appreciate your specifying the objection. Under the circumstances, and pending any information from you, I do not see what action I can take and cannot comply with the request contained in the second paragraph of your letter.

I am pleased to see in your statement that you desire to play baseball in 1970. I take it this puts to rest any thought, as reported earlier in the press, that you were considering retirement.
Sincerely yours,
Bowie Kuhn

Although nothing was said explicitly in either letter about legal action, press accounts over the following days assumed the inevitability of a court hearing. The *Sporting News*, for example, headlined its January 3 story: "Flood in Town, Baseball Suit Will Follow" and ten days later featured an editorial describing the situation as "on a collision course." A New York paper referred to Flood's letter as a "prelude" to legal action. In fact, several meetings were held before and after Flood received Kuhn's letter, attended by Flood; Miller; Miller's assistant Dick Moss; Kuhn; Goldberg; and Jay Topkis, a lawyer in Goldberg's firm. Although the purpose of these meetings was ostensibly to explore the possibility of a negotiated resolution of Flood's situation, accounts of the meetings by the participants suggest an atmosphere hardly conducive to a compromise settlement. In his memoir, *Hardball: The Education of a Baseball Commissioner*, Bowie Kuhn complained that although he had anticipated dealing with Marvin Miller, Goldberg "did most of the talking" and "took an inflexible position." After Goldberg had "sailed off," Kuhn wondered if the former justice "had not somehow managed to top even my well-honed reputation for pomposity." In Curt Flood's version of these meetings, it was the baseball owners who "rejected" attempts to resolve the situation through negotiation and Goldberg who deftly parried Kuhn's "cat and mouse" attempts to make it appear as if Flood was being inflexible. At one point Flood recalled the commissioner asking if negotiation was useless and if "the suit will proceed regardless." At that, "Goldberg took him [Kuhn] apart." "It is my understanding," shot back the former justice, "that if appropriate modifications can be made through negotiation, they would satisfy Curt Flood. Therefore, if you want to carry out your legal right to negotiate, please do so."

That each side may have had cause to suspect the other of coming to these meetings in less than a spirit of good faith is suggested by another curious inconsistency in the accounts of Kuhn, Miller, and Flood. Kuhn wrote that he had also been in Puerto Rico for the Players Association meeting and had met with the executive board and Miller on December 14, the day after Flood's appearance. He claimed that nothing had been discussed with him that day about Flood's intentions or the association's decision to support Flood's legal action. Although Miller made no mention of the commissioner's participation in Puerto Rico, an appendix in Curt Flood's autobiography, *The Way It Is*, consists of "an accurate reproduction of the notes taken at the meeting" under the title "Discussion with Commissioner Bowie K. Kuhn at Major-League Baseball Players Association Executive Board Meeting, December 14, 1969, San Juan, Puerto Rico." According to these "notes," Kuhn and the board talked about a number of issues such as earflaps on batting helmets, artificial playing surfaces, even the venues for future association meetings. But indeed, nothing was said about Flood or the reserve clause issue!

In retrospect, then, the press focus on the inevitability of a legal contest was not entirely misplaced. Both sides had already begun a campaign of public commentary and media interviews intended to demonstrate their seriousness of purpose and respective dedication to the best interests of the sport. Flood and Miller gave such interviews and appeared on television and radio broadcasts. At the same time, the presidents of the two leagues, Joe Cronin of the American and Charles

"Chub" Feeney of the National, issued a joint public statement accusing Flood, "a highly paid star," of refusing to honor the terms of his players' contract. Their statement also expressed "regret" at the support given Flood by the Players Association and went on to catalog the likely harmful results if Flood were to succeed. They concluded that the sport of professional baseball "would simply cease to exist."

As with any sporting contest, the press, the public, and many of those directly involved in baseball began choosing sides and making known their support or opposition to Flood's challenge. At least up until the trial, Flood would complain that "comparatively few newspaper, radio, and television journalists seemed able to understand what I was doing" and that much of the commentary that he was aware of "was distressingly cynical and ill-informed." He singled out a number of writers, however, who he did feel were attempting to be "fair" in their reporting. One such supporter was the sports columnist for the *New York Times*, Leonard Koppett, who beginning in January would write a series of articles and opinion pieces critical of baseball and its treatment of Flood.

At the same time, those in the media and press whom Flood referred to as "myopic" were not necessarily completely supportive fans of the reserve clause and the owners. Rather, especially at the outset of the case, they questioned Flood's personal motives and methods as much as his cause. One such example was Bob Broeg, the respected sports editor of the *St. Louis Post-Dispatch*. In early February, Broeg wrote a piece in the *Post-Dispatch*, reprinted elsewhere, called "Just What Prompted Flood Lawsuit?" He began his article by stating that "sympathy" for a challenge to baseball's reserve clause would be "considerably greater" if the clause were being contested by "a player less affluent than Flood." In Broeg's version of the reserve clause story, it was the ballplayers who had been "held down and kept back" who had been most harmed by the reserve system, and he cited the stories of several players, including Fred Bennett and Harry "the Cat" Brecheen, from earlier decades to illustrate his point. Flood, in contrast, had "benefitted from a large measure of personal considerations," especially the support of Cardinals president Gussie Busch. For Broeg, Flood's lawsuit was "not a matter of principle, but of principal," and to prove his point, Broeg questioned why Flood had asked for the $75,000 in damages named in his suit. If Flood was truly doing this for the "principle," then he "would have asked for $1 in damages and the right to negotiate for himself." Broeg concluded his piece with some choice sarcasm, noting that Flood's legal brief had "more errors in it than Curt ever made" and echoing the owners' claim that the "integrity" of baseball itself would be harmed if Flood were to succeed, since it would mean that a player while "playing with one club" could be negotiating to play with another club the following season.

On Friday, January 16, 1970, attorneys Goldberg and Zerman filed suit on behalf of "Curtis C. Flood" in the U.S. District Court for the Southern District of New York. Named as respondents in the seventeen-page complaint were Bowie Kuhn, "individually and as Commissioner of Baseball"; the presidents of the two leagues, Charles S. Feeney of the National and Joseph E. Cronin of the American; and all twenty-four professional Major League Baseball teams. The complaint detailed five "causes of action," that is, the wrongful acts that the respondents/defendants allegedly committed. The first three claims involved baseball's "reserve system" allowing St. Louis to trade Flood with or without his approval. This system, it was alleged, constituted a "conspiracy" on the part of all named defendants in violation of federal antitrust laws, specifically the Sherman Antitrust Act. Moreover, it was charged that this conspiracy had resulted in significant "damage" to the plaintiff, for which he was asking for "treble damages" totaling $75,000. The complaint also asked the court to issue a "preliminary injunction" stopping the defendants from enforcing the reserve clause against Flood so that he could continue to play baseball while the suit was pending. In the event that this request was denied, the complaint asked the court to award $3 million in additional damages. The fourth "cause of action" contended that the defendants were engaged in a conspiracy to "subject plaintiff to peonage and involuntary servitude" in violation of federal laws and the Thirteenth Amendment to the Constitution.

The fifth and final "cause of action" was somewhat curious, since it did not relate directly to either Flood's trade or the reserve system. It charged that two ball clubs, the St. Louis Cardinals and the New York Yankees, had each engaged in activities that violated federal and state antitrust laws, "thereby causing irreparable injury to plaintiff and the public." The activities in question were the sale of beer at the St. Louis stadium and the ownership of the Yankees team by the Columbia Broadcasting System. In the former instance, it was claimed that the Cardinals were owned by a company engaged in "the production, distribution and sale of beer," and that in limiting the concession sale of beer in the St. Louis ballpark to its own product, the company was increasing its revenues while decreasing the team's revenue that presumably would be available for players' salaries. In the latter case, it was argued that CBS's ownership of the Yankees prevented competitive bidding from the other two national networks for broadcasting rights to professional baseball games, resulting in reduced revenues to be shared by all the teams for use in paying players' salaries.

The following week, the first hearing was held in federal court before Judge Dudley B. Bonsal. At the hearing, the owners asked for, and were granted, an additional two weeks to prepare their reply. Although neither Flood nor Kuhn was present at the hearing, an attorney representing the Philadelphia Phillies baseball team informed Judge Bonsal of the Phillies' willingness to have Flood report for the team's spring training, due to start the following month, and to "play without prejudice" while the case was going on. Flood's counsel Jay Topkis replied, "That's exactly what he doesn't want to do. . . . He lives in St. Louis, has a business there and doesn't want to be treated like cattle."

On February 3, a second hearing was held, this time before Judge Irving Ben Cooper. Judge Cooper had been appointed by President John F. Kennedy in 1962 to a newly created seat for the Southern District. Prior to his elevation to the federal bench, he had served from 1939 to 1960 as associate justice and then as chief justice of the New York Court of Special Sessions. Judge Cooper had received his law degree from Washington University in St. Louis in 1939. He was known for being outspoken and controversial, and at the time of his appointment in 1962, *Time* magazine wrote that he was known as "a temperamental tyrant who threw tantrums on the bench." The magazine also noted that his nomination had been opposed by both the American Bar Association and the New York County Lawyers Association.

At the hearing, attorneys for both Flood and baseball raised many of the arguments they would make all the way up to the Supreme Court. However, the immediate concern was the plaintiff's request for a court order — the preliminary injunction — that would enable

Flood to negotiate with other teams to play in the upcoming season. Goldberg compared his client to a "high-priced slave" who had decided that "he cannot play under an illegal system . . . [and] he's not willing to be sold into servitude." He pointed out that professional football did not have the same exemption from antitrust laws as baseball yet "seemed to be doing very well" and repeated Flood's claim that the suit was not "designed to cripple or harass baseball." In response, Mark F. Hughes, representing the baseball owners, and Paul Porter, representing the commissioner, contended that if the court were to issue an injunction, as the plaintiff wanted, it would be "very grave, to the point of being catastrophic." In an exchange reminiscent of the earlier presuit negotiating sessions, Hughes offered Flood the opportunity to play for the Phillies in the upcoming season "without prejudicing his suit." Flood countered by expressing his willingness to play the next season with the Cardinals "with or without a contract" until the case was decided.

One month later, on March 4, Judge Cooper announced his decision in the matter of *Flood v. Kuhn, et al.* Although the opinion discussed all the claims made by Flood involving the reserve clause, the "sole question" specifically ruled on at this time was the issuance of the preliminary injunction against Kuhn and the owners. For Judge Cooper, the injunction issue was entirely "a matter of law." In denying the plaintiff's motion for such a court order, he cited both the various prior judicial rulings that had upheld baseball's reserve clause and the defendants' arguments that issuing such an injunction would be tantamount to deciding the case without a trial on the factual claims made by both parties. He conceded that professional ballplayers "have chafed under the restrictions of baseball's reserve system" and that "many of their grievances appear justified." Yet, he concluded, to issue an injunction at this point would "work the type of unfair surprise and carry the same sort of sudden effect" that earlier precedents had precluded. Accordingly, the judge ruled that the "determination" of the issues presented "must at least be the result of a full trial and not on the basis of a motion for preliminary relief."

Judge Cooper concluded his opinion denying the injunction with an observation that suggested (correctly, as it turned out) his underlying sympathies and the inordinate emotion when baseball entered the courtroom:

Baseball has been the national pastime for over one hundred years and enjoys a unique place in our American heritage. Major League Professional Baseball is avidly followed by millions of fans, looked upon with fervor and pride and provides a special source of inspiration and competitive team spirit especially for the young. Baseball's status in the life of the nation is so pervasive that it would not strain credulity to say the court can take judicial notice that baseball is everybody's business. To put it mildly and with restraint, it would be unfortunate indeed if a fine sport and profession, which brings surcease from daily travail and an escape from the ordinary to most inhabitants of this land, were to suffer in the least because of undue concentration by any one or any group on commercial and profit considerations.

The game is on higher ground; it behooves everyone to keep it there.

Flood's attorneys chose not to appeal Judge Cooper's ruling, believing that such a move would only delay the case unnecessarily. Accordingly, on April 11, the judge set a date for the trial to begin — May 18. Already Miller's and Goldberg's predictions of a long, drawn-out fight were proving wrong. The case seemed to be proceeding at a very un-legal-like pace. At both the February 3 hearing and in his decision on the preliminary injunction, Judge Cooper displayed what would become an ongoing penchant on his part for resorting to baseball terminology and sports allusions in his courtroom comments as well as his rulings. At the hearing he announced: "You've thrown the ball to me. I hope I don't muff it." He then made reference to an earlier Supreme Court opinion in which a judge was likened to "an umpire who calls them as he sees them." In his decision on the motion for injunctive relief, he wrote of the possibility that the "grip" of the reserve system "may well be far too tight and it may be best to loosen the bonds without permitting the slightest sag to the body of the game." And if there was any doubt, at least in Judge Cooper's mind, that the confluence of bar, bench, and ball field had begun, the judge concluded his ruling by pointing out to both sides that this was, after all, only the "first inning."

"Your Grandfather and I"

During a television appearance on the *Dick Cavett Show* in early January, Curt Flood was asked to explain his decision to sue baseball. He responded by noting that "there is nothing more damaging to a person's ego as a human being than to be traded or bought and sold like a piece of property." When reminded that as a ballplayer he had been "pretty well paid," Flood shot back: "A well-paid slave is nonetheless a slave." The newspaper account of the interview the following day featured the headline "90G Still Slavery, Sez Flood." Aside from his reference to himself as having been treated as "property" in his letter to the commissioner, this was perhaps the first but by no means the last time in public that Flood would link his situation and cause with his race and the nation's "peculiar institution" of slavery that had defined African Americans for centuries. Indeed, in Curt Flood's many press and media interviews and appearances during and long after his case ended he would be even more explicit, comparing himself to the nineteenth-century African American slave Dred Scott, whose unsuccessful lawsuit for freedom in the 1850s had been a factor in the beginning of the Civil War. Not surprisingly, one of the legal arguments raised by Flood's attorneys in his lawsuit would question the constitutionality of the reserve system under the Thirteenth Amendment, which had abolished slavery at the end of that conflict.

In one sense, Flood's comparison of his struggle with that of the slave Dred Scott seemed appropriate. Both men were African Americans who attempted to use the American legal system to gain — unsuccessfully, as it turned out — their "freedom" as they understood that term. At the same time, as will be seen, there were those both outside and within the African American community who were concerned about a person of Flood's recognized achievements — and salary — invoking the name of a man who, if not for the case that bears his name, would have been invisible on the pages of history. Yet however accurate or appropriate Flood's comparison may or may not have been, for a historian, one thing is clear. From the countless articles written about him in newspapers and magazines; the many radio and television interviews he gave; and especially his 1971 autobiography, *The Way It Is*, far more is known about Curt Flood's life before, during, and after his legal fight than will ever be gleaned about the man whose earlier case came to symbolize the struggle over slavery in America.

Curtis Charles Flood was born in Houston, Texas, on January 18, 1938, the youngest of six children born to Laura and Herman Flood. Two years later, the family moved to Oakland, California, where the tremendous expansion of Bay-area port and naval facilities leading up to the U.S. entry into World War II had created what was characterized as a "second gold rush" of job opportunities. In spite of his parents both working multiple jobs, Flood would describe his early condition by saying: "We were not poor, but we had nothing. That is, we ate at regular intervals, but not much." The recollected vision of his childhood in Oakland was that of a "conventionally squalid ghetto" with the "usual" debris — garbage-strewn streets, bars, prostitutes, drunks, pushers, and "thoughtless violence." Although his parents could harbor the aspirations of the classic American dream for their family — a nice home, a job, education — Flood understood from an early age that it was the allure and dangers of those streets that mattered more to the lives and future of young African Americans. At the age of ten, Flood would have what he called his "first and final" run-in with the law, taking an unlocked truck for a two-block ride that landed him in a juvenile detention center for a night. Flood's older brother Carl would not be so fortunate and would spend much of the rest of his life in trouble with the law.

Looking back on his early life, Flood expressed frustration at the "idiotic comparisons" between the experience of growing up African American and that of European immigrants, especially those who had become "tired" of feeling guilty about what "their grandfathers did to my grandfathers." "To hell with your grandfather, baby," Flood would write. "Just get out of my way." Yet his escape from the Oakland ghetto, where few whites could be found "and none were the bearer of joy," was aided by several white men who may or may not have shared the guilt, or lack thereof, about which Flood wrote. What they did share was a genuine recognition that Curt Flood possessed talents and the character and personality to do something with those talents. The three men were Jim Chambers, Sam Bercovich, and George Powles.

Jim Chambers was Flood's high school art teacher, a self-described "free spirit" who recognized his student's genuine talent and nourished what would become a lifelong passion for portraiture. Even after Flood chose a career in baseball, his artistic talents would be heralded along with his ballplaying accomplishments. The *Sporting News* described him as "A Rembrandt Off Diamond" who "paints portraits the way he plays ball. Fast. Smooth. With perfection." Another feature article showed a drawing of a staff artist drawing a portrait of Flood as a Cardinal, Flood standing next to him, with the caption "mind if I give you a few pointers??" The article described Flood as having "a great pair of hands both in the outfield and at the drawing board . . . he can swing the brush as well as the bat." The high point, as it were, of his artistic career came in the wake of the assassination of Dr. Martin Luther King Jr. in April 1968. As a tribute to a man he deeply admired and as a "personal token" to Dr. King's widow, Coretta Scott King, Flood painted a portrait of the slain civil rights leader that would hang in the living room of Mrs. King's Atlanta home.

By far the most important influences on Flood's early baseball career were Sam Bercovich and George Powles. Bercovich owned an Oakland furniture store, where Flood worked after school. Bercovich was also a longtime and enthusiastic sports backer of both professional teams (he was friends with Oakland sports magnate Al Davis) and local amateur leagues. He introduced Flood to George Powles, a high school coach who spent his summers working with youth baseball leagues in Oakland's public parks. Powles, "a squat, middle-aged white man with a buzz cut," embodied the essential qualities of the many individuals working in public parks across America in the postwar years. He loved baseball and kids and believed that ability and effort were more important than skin color. "He neither preached nor patronized," Flood remembered, and his success in encouraging and developing future greats is evidenced by the roster of star athletes who, like Flood, played for him, such as Frank Robinson, Vada Pinson, Billy Martin, Joe Morgan, and even basketball legend Bill Russell. It was

Powles who convinced Flood that, despite his relatively small stature at five feet seven inches and 140 pounds, he could play professional baseball. With characteristic honesty, Powles also advised Flood to "steel himself" to the fact that his size would not be the only barrier to a successful career. Black ballplayers had to outperform their white counterparts and even then could not expect equal recognition or rewards.

Upon graduating from high school in 1955, Flood had to choose between a career in commercial art or baseball. It was an "easy" choice. He met a scouting contact through Powles and was signed to a one-year contract with the Cincinnati Reds, receiving a $4,000 annual salary. In February 1956, Flood left California, traveling to Tampa, Florida, for the Reds' spring training camp. In Florida he experienced, as did other African American players during these years, what biographer Alex Belth termed genuine "culture shock." The Supreme Court had directly struck down "separate but equal" policies in its 1954 *Brown v. Board of Education* decision, but the South in the 1950s was still largely a place where "Jim Crow" racial segregation prevailed, and in the 1950s Major League Baseball teams conducted their spring training in the South. Flood recalled his first encounter with drinking fountains for "whites" and "coloreds," and instead of staying with his Reds teammates at a nice hotel, he was forced to take his room and board with other black players at Ma Fielders, a local boardinghouse outside town.

After a short time, Flood was assigned to one of the Reds' minor league "farm teams," the High Point–Thomasville, North Carolina, "Hi-Toms." There he endured constant abuse and indignities, both off and on the field, yet he managed to keep his cool, performing well enough to be called up to the Reds toward the end of the 1956 season. Significantly, in recounting a meeting he had with the Reds' general manager, Gabe Paul, during the final days of that season, Flood was well aware that "the Reds now had exclusive rights to my baseball services for as long as they chose to retain them. I could play only where they elected to send me. This was baseball law. It was beyond question or dispute. It was taken entirely for granted." As if he needed confirmation of how professional baseball operated, during the winter prior to the 1958 season, Paul informed Flood that he had been traded to the St. Louis Cardinals. In 1970 reporters and sportswriters would point out that Flood had made no protest at the time of this, his first trade, implying that his lawsuit thirteen years later, after his second trade, was "freshly minted, opportunistic and inconsistent." Flood's answer to that charge would be to claim that he didn't sue "because the possibility didn't even occur to me. If it had, I would not have dared to act on it."

Like many of Flood's remarks, his later explanation for going along with this first trade has a cryptic quality in that it doesn't really address the charge that his "attitudes" had somehow changed over the years. If the reserve system was wrong in 1970, why was it not equally wrong in 1957? In that sense, Flood's lawsuit was "inconsistent," but not necessarily in the way reporters and commentators saw it. In 1957 Curt Flood was an unproven rookie ballplayer, and it had become evident that his future opportunities were limited simply by the Reds' having established players at the field positions Flood could play. Moreover, the Cardinals offered him a $5,000 yearly salary, which as he himself noted, was a 25 percent increase. For a rookie ballplayer in 1957, that was a significant raise and salary, in which case his *inaction* in 1957 was more likely "opportunistic" than hypocritical.

It is also the case that in 1957, the St. Louis Cardinals baseball franchise had its own selfish reasons for wanting the young player. The Cardinals had been one of the oldest teams in the National League and could trace its lineage back to the 1870s. But it was not until 1926 that the team managed to win its first league title and its first World Series. Thereafter it became one of baseball's more successful franchises, winning seven National League pennants between 1930 and 1946 and five World Series crowns. A major reason for this success was the 1919 hiring of Branch Rickey to be the team's general manager. It was Rickey who came up with the "ingenious" idea of using minor league teams as a "farm system" to provide his club with a steady supply of talented players. "I would find them young," he claimed, "but I could find them and develop them. Pick them from the sandlots and keep them until they became stars." And Rickey could keep them because these young players would be required to sign contracts with the minor league clubs that "reserved" their services until such time as the team might trade them; release them; or, hopefully for the player, send them "up" to the majors.

By the early 1950s, however, the Cardinals were no longer considered a baseball powerhouse. Branch Rickey had left the club in 1946 to take a similar position with the Brooklyn Dodgers, where he would cap his Hall of Fame career by signing the first African American major leaguer, Jackie Robinson. In 1954 the Cardinals were bought by the Anheuser-Busch Company, the St. Louis brewer of Budweiser beer. The company's president, August "Gussie" Busch, had made the brewery one of the most profitable in the area; like one of the first owners of the St. Louis franchise, brewer Chris Van Der Ahe, Gussie Busch saw a baseball team as a way to sell more beer — and a good baseball team that attracted larger crowds would sell more beer. Part of Busch's strategy involved using his deep pockets to purchase, unsuccessfully, quality players from other teams. He went through a series of managers and general managers, finally settling on Fred Hutchinson, a former Major League pitcher, and Vaughn "Bing" Devine, to guide the team on and off the field respectively. It seemed to work: In 1957 the Cardinals finished a surprising second in the standings. Off the field, the "cautious, deliberate" Devine attempted to provide the players to bring the Cardinals back to "respectability."

Gussie Busch also believed the Cardinals "needed" black players. Before the Brooklyn Dodgers moved to Los Angeles in 1957, St. Louis was the farthest western and *southern* baseball franchise in the Major Leagues. In many ways the city had been, and continued to be, a southern town in which racial segregation and discrimination were widespread even if not legally sanctioned, as in the rest of the South. Yet it seems likely that Busch's decision to integrate his baseball team was made less from any racial sensitivities than from more selfish economic reasons. As Flood biographer Alex Belth concluded, not having African Americans on the team made little sense. "After all many of the people who bought Budweiser were black. Why alienate those customers? It wasn't good business." To secure such players, Busch first tried the buying strategy mentioned above: His offers to purchase two African American all-star players, Willie Mays of the Giants and Ernie Banks of the Cubs, were both rejected. Busch then ordered his staff to "go out and find our own players."

By the start of the 1954 season, the Cardinals had signed their first two African American players, Tom Alston and Brooks Lawrence. Alston, a first baseman and promising hitter from San Diego, "didn't work out." According to Bing Devine, Alston "had a lot of problems, most of which I can't be specific about, except to say he was troubled." By July Alston had been exiled to the Rochester minor league team, where he languished for three years before leaving the game for good. The other black player, pitcher Brooks Lawrence, fared somewhat better. He finished that first season with a very respectable record of 15 wins and 6 losses. But the following season, he developed an ulcer and ultimately found himself being sent to the minors. Eventually he was traded to Cincinnati, where he had several successful years until arm problems forced his retirement in 1960.

In Peter Golenboch's oral history of the Cardinals, *The Spirit of St. Louis*, Lawrence spoke movingly and candidly of his experience as one of the first African American players for the Cardinals. Upon graduating from high school in Zanesville, Ohio, in 1943, Lawrence joined the military. The only place where he didn't encounter segregation was playing ball. After he left the military, he used the G.I. Bill to study at Miami University of Ohio. After two years, he left school to sign with the Cleveland Indians and for the next five years played with a variety of minor league clubs until being traded to St. Louis. Lawrence's commentary confirmed the racial divide that characterized St. Louis during these years. He admitted that the whole time he lived in St. Louis, he "didn't go downtown more than twice. There wasn't anything downtown for me. They wouldn't let me in the restaurants, wouldn't let me in any of those public places." Naturally, he and Alston had to room together, and he reported that the two never ventured far from their boardinghouse. When the team left the city by train, he always had to wait in the "colored" waiting room even though "they knew who we were."

What also emerges from Lawrence's recollections is the isolation and loneliness he and Alston felt, compounded by the pressures of constant media and public scrutiny of the "first" African American Cardinals. "I was not friends with anyone on the club," he recalled, and during his entire time with the team he never spoke with Harry Caray, the team's broadcaster. This isolation obviously took its toll, both in Alston's "troubles" and Lawrence's bleeding ulcer. Interestingly, Curt Flood would later comment in his autobiography on the many professional ballplayers who developed "stomach difficulties" or other ailments that had to be ignored or hidden for fear of ending one's career, and the price paid by those players in terms of personal and family problems off the field.

Curt Flood played his first Major League game with the St. Louis Cardinals on May 2, 1958, against the same Cincinnati team that had traded him away the winter before. Unlike Lawrence, who had had to labor for several seasons in the minors before his first Major League appearance, Flood spent less than three weeks with the Cardinals' Omaha minor league franchise before being called up to the majors. But Flood would spend much of the rest of the season on the bench, and while his hitting proved a "pleasant surprise," he was valued more for his defensive skills and baserunning ability. It didn't help that as a team, the Cardinals fared poorly that season, ending up in fifth place. Since this was not the kind of respectability owner Gussie Busch was seeking, someone had to be held accountable. At the close of the season, Busch fired Fred Hutchinson. Hutchinson, or "Hutch," was liked and respected by the players, including Flood.

That was not necessarily the case with his successor, Solly Hemus. Flood's statistics over the next two and a half seasons reflect his continuing status as only a sometime starter. The number of games Flood played in did not increase much, his times at bat actually dropped, and his batting average was by no means impressive. He believed that players of lesser talent were being used by Hemus — more to the point, these players were all white. He never called Hemus a racist, but Flood remembered several incidents in which the manager referred to an opposing player as a "black son of a bitch." He was also angered by Hemus's belittling treatment of an African American teammate, Hall of Fame pitcher Bob Gibson. "Until then we [Flood, Gibson, and two other black players, Bill White and George Crowe] had detested Hemus for not using his best lineup. Now we hated him for himself." Flood claimed that it was Hemus's behavior that started him thinking about the unequal treatment of African American ballplayers generally. Baseball may have become integrated, but "the black [player] had to be better than a white of equal experience, or he would be shown the door." Exclusion was no longer the issue; unequal treatment certainly was, and for the young player, Hemus was an example of baseball's racism "showing. Outstanding blacks get jobs. Lesser blacks are shunted aside in favor of whites, sometimes to the detriment of the team. The mistake of Solly Hemus was not that he misused and mistreated blacks but that he overdid it."

It was not only Flood who struggled with Hemus's leadership. The Cardinals had done better in 1960, but by the middle of the 1961 season, the team was again struggling, and "Mighty Mouse," as he was called, was gone. His replacement, Johnny Keane, changed everything. Keane had been Flood's minor league coach and was one of the Cardinals' coaches when he was named manager. In both earlier roles he had been a consistent believer in Flood's potential, and the day after he became manager, Flood started playing center field regularly. Flood and the team "would never look back." As Flood himself admitted, under Keane's (and his successor Red Schoendienst's) leadership, "I did my thing." Success in baseball is measured by the "stats," the numerical output of a player's batting, fielding, or pitching, and Curt Flood's stats over the next seven seasons justified Keane's faith in him. He batted over .300 six times, and in 1967 his .335 average was the fourth highest in the National League. Despite several poor seasons, Flood's career batting average would be a respectable .293. In terms of Cardinals team numbers, including players since 1970, Flood is sixth in total number of games played (1,769), seventh in total at-bats (6,318), eighth in total hits (1,853), and twelfth in doubles (271).

Flood's record as a fielder was even more impressive. During his entire career as a center fielder, his fielding percentage (chances versus errors) never went below the ninetieth percentile, and he completed the 1966 season without a single fielding error (in 396 chances). From 1963 to 1969, he won consecutive Golden Glove Awards, an award given to the outstanding fielder at that position in the league that season, and his overall excellence was recognized by his selection three times (1964, 1966, and 1968) for the National League's all-star team. His prowess and leadership abilities were also recognized by his fellow Cardinals players, who elected him team captain each season from 1965 to 1969; a team press release in July 1968 referred to Flood as "the dean of the Cardinals at only 30." The statement provided a vivid description of the center fielder and his style of play:

> At first glance, you find it difficult to believe Curt Flood could be anything but a professional entertainer, like a dancer or singer. He carries only 160 pounds on his 5-foot-9 frame, is not particularly

broad through the chest and shoulders, and as he emerges from a ballpark following a baseball game, mixing with the likes of Orlando Cepeda, Mike Shannon and Steve Carlton, he almost looks out of place. Flood is an entertainer, of course, but he performs on a baseball field, and there are few players around today who play the game as well as he does. Put Flood in centerfield and watch his lightning takeoff at the crack of the bat, his charge toward the outfield wall, and finally, the spectacular leaping catch, so reminiscent of the ones that have filled his career. Or put him at the plate and watch the level, picturesque swing that has produced more than 1,580 major league hits.

Although the language might be read as the usual publicity department hyperbole, that image of Curt Flood on the field would be confirmed in countless newspaper and magazine articles. From the local St. Louis media to such national periodicals as the *Sporting News* and *Sports Illustrated*, the essential elements of Flood's baseball persona appear repeatedly: his relatively small stature, his speed and grace, and his consistency and reliability in all aspects of the game. The special "opening day issue" of the *Sporting News* on April 12, 1969, featured a full-cover picture of Flood along with fellow Cardinals outfielders Lou Brock and Vada Pinson. Displayed above Flood's head in bold print was the word "SPEED."

Flood's success as a player coincided with the return of the Cardinals team to the kind of respectability that owner Gussie Busch had been seeking. During the 1960s the St. Louis Cardinals once again became a National League powerhouse. In 1964, in a pennant race that came down to the last game of the season, the Cardinals won their first National League title since 1946. They went on to defeat the legendary New York Yankees for the world championship in a thrilling seven-game World Series. Three years later they captured the 1967 National League title in convincing fashion, beating the second-place San Francisco Giants by ten and a half games. In another seven-game World Series, they beat the Boston Red Sox, who had accomplished their own "impossible dream" by winning the American League title on the last day of the season. The next year the Cardinals again won the league title easily but were ambushed by the underdog Detroit Tigers, who came from a two-game deficit to win the last three games in a row and the world championship. Overall, the decade of the 1960s was one of the best for the Cardinals, with a combined record of 884 wins and 718 losses. It was much better than the preceding decade, before Flood's arrival, and even more so than the 1970s, after his departure.

But the numbers were not the entire story of Curt Flood and the Cardinals during what one writer called these "championship years." The statistics do not explain the sometimes intangible yet very real aspects of a team sport like baseball, such as the relationships between the players themselves or the "spirit" or cohesiveness of the team on and especially off the field. Such statistics do not account for the personal lives and experiences of the players when not at "work" (as Flood himself called it), nor do they readily reveal the larger societal issues and developments within which the game and business of baseball function. The years during which the Cardinals were winning their championships coincided with the "turbulent" decade of the 1960s — an era of the Vietnam War; "sex, drugs, and rock and roll"; and, most importantly, issues of race.

By 1967 Flood was praising his team for its "camaraderie," its spirit, and especially its freedom from any "racist poison." Nelson Briles, a white pitcher for the Cardinals during these years, confirmed that "we went out together as a team. We played hard together on the field as a team. We won as a team, lost as a team, and it was nothing to see white and black and Latino players out afterward." But Flood was equally quick to point out that such unity had not always been the case and that the cohesiveness that developed, especially between the white and black players, had resulted from the efforts of the African American players, notably Bob Gibson and Flood himself. "It began with Gibson and me deliberately kicking over traditional barriers to establish communication with the palefaces." As a result of these efforts, "actual friendships developed." Going out together after games to local jazz clubs favored by Gibson, Flood, and another all-star black outfielder, Lou Brock, was one way in which the "strangeness" between the two races was bridged. But with his usual candor, Flood also admitted to more traditional methods of male bonding: "Those of us with a taste for the joys of the night swapped booze and chicks from one end of the country to the other."

Flood soon settled into life in St. Louis, with an apartment and a sports car, and sought out the restaurants and jazz clubs in the city more readily than the first black players on the Cardinals, Alston and Lawrence, had seemed able or willing to do. In 1959 he met and married Beverly Collins, an eighteen-year-old local beauty whose parents owned a "walk-up" restaurant that Flood frequented. At the time of their marriage, Beverly was a divorced mother of two young children, Debbie and Gary. Flood would adopt both, and over the next several years the couple would have three more children, Curt Jr., Shelly, and finally Scott. The two seemed to live the lifestyle of most professional baseball couples, with Beverly involved in the various charity and social events expected of players' wives at the time. In 1962 Flood's former art teacher Jim Chambers introduced him to a white couple, Marian and John, or "Johnny." The Jorgensens would become for Flood "closer than friends, freer and easier than family." Their wide-ranging interests and "powerful goodness," as Flood put it, would have a tremendous impact on his life. Johnny got Flood involved in his Oakland engraving business, and the younger man was instantly drawn in by the combination of his artistic talent and his enjoyment of the "infinite detail of close work." Flood also appreciated the fact that Johnny trusted him enough to make him a partner in the business, yet never pressured him to give up his baseball career. Eventually Flood would use this experience to set up his own photography and portrait business in St. Louis.

By 1968 it seemed as though Curt Flood was indeed doing his "thing." He was an all-star player on a championship team, and his performance on the field was on a trajectory likely to earn him admittance to the Baseball Hall of Fame in Cooperstown, New York. He had a family, caring and supportive friends, and the beginnings of a successful off-season business. It seemed he was living a "version of the American dream" that his parents had once envisioned for him. Yet for a historian attempting to explain the when and how of an important legal case, there is an obligation to try to make clear the motivations and the "whys." In Curt Flood's case, there is ample evidence, much of it from Flood himself, suggesting that the story of his decision to not accept his trade and play for Philadelphia, and then to sue baseball, was more complex and certainly not as surprising as it appeared to many at the time.

In 1971 Flood published his autobiography/memoir, *The Way It Is*, and perhaps nowhere is this complexity better suggested than on the book's dust jacket. On the front, under Curt Flood's name, is a picture of a baseball resting on grass. But the seams of the ball have been torn out, with a sagging flap exposing the inside core of the ball. The back is even more remarkable, for instead of the usual picture of the author of a sports memoir in uniform, Flood is wearing formal attire, a business suit, complete with French cuffs and cufflinks. He is shown in a close-up, hunched slightly forward, with his hands folded together almost touching his chin. He is not looking at the camera but slightly down and away, and his expression is serious and thoughtful. He looks, in short, not like an athlete but like someone sitting at a courtroom table intently listening to his past and future being argued and debated. The only evidence of his identity as a baseball player is the championship ring he wears. The photo stands in stark contrast to the many pictures of Flood taken during the years up to 1969, in which he is shown either in action on the ball field or standing still, most often smiling in a way that suggests someone who genuinely enjoys what he is doing and has succeeded in doing it. Even the book's promotional blurb is suggestive, describing the book as "scarcely . . . a baseball book at all."

Yet *The Way It Is* most certainly was about baseball and Curt Flood's life in the game. The book is brutally honest in a way that sports memoirs had not been until that time (although now such frankness and honest self-analysis on the part of the athlete-writer is the rule, not the exception). Like the baseball on the book jacket, it exposes what Flood believed was the inner core of the game and those involved in its operation. It was not an especially pretty picture. In one chapter, appropriately titled "Geniuses Need Not Apply," he detailed the intellectual shortcomings and limitations of those, especially the managers, who run professional teams. "Some mighty dim people," he concluded, "have become quite successful managers." In another chapter Flood described what he called the "national pastime's pastime": sex. For young, healthy, and "randy" ballplayers, there existed a plentiful supply of available women who were more than willing to provide a needed "therapeutic" release after a tough day or night at the ballpark. According to Flood, sex for players was the "ultimate remedy" for the intense pressures of the game, second only to the pharmacopeia of drugs his fellow players carried with them. At the same time, he confessed that such behavior created additional problems and tensions for players, especially those like himself who were married and had families. Flood would ultimately divorce, remarry, and then separate a second time from his wife, Beverly, and he recognized that the life of a ballplayer, with its days on the road and different hours, made it difficult for him to be a good father.

The sex, drugs, and ignorant managers were part of Flood's portrait of baseball, but by no means the whole picture. Although Flood could brag about the "beautiful unity" of the players on the championship teams of the 1960s, it is clear that for him the specter and impact of racism in years before and after only highlighted how unique and perhaps fragile that unity and spirit were. He was equally aware that the fortunes of a professional baseball player can turn in an instant, often for the worse. An injury or illness, even personal problems, and a single mistake can mean the end of a career. This reality was made all the more hazardous by the fact that the front-office people, from owners down to managers, tended to operate on the basis of whim, with no fixed or consistent set of standards or expectations. The "instant" in Curt Flood's case may have been a single play in the last game of the 1968 World Series. After a slow start during the 1968 season, the Cardinals had a fairly easy time winning the National League championship. Flood had a good year, winning another Golden Glove and making the league's all-star team. Although his batting average was .301, in a year dominated by outstanding pitchers, it was enough to place him fifth out of all National League batters at the season's end. The Cardinals' opponents were the Detroit Tigers, who, thanks to their 31-game-winning pitcher Mickey Lolich, had captured the American League crown in convincing fashion. Even though the Tigers were considered the underdogs in the World Series, they managed to force the Cardinals to a seventh and deciding game. In the seventh inning of a scoreless game, Flood misjudged a fly ball that normally he would have had little problem in catching. Several runs scored, and Detroit went on to win the game and the World Series.

Flood's teammates refused to blame him for the loss. As professionals, they certainly understood how much of the game is a matter of split seconds and inches, and how even the best players can make a mistake even at the most crucial moments. But media commentators, especially the local St. Louis writers, were not so understanding.

Rather than directly criticizing any individual's specific mistake or poor performance on the field, they focused instead on a broader and touchier issue: the players' salaries. The Cardinals, ironically having recently been characterized as "the world's most expensive team," were now cast as a prime example of the most serious problem facing professional baseball — overpaid players. It was a revival of an issue and a theme that, as will be examined in the following chapters, was as old as professional baseball itself. By 1968 it was clear that baseball, whatever else it was to the most loyal and passionate fans and commentators, was a business. The players were employees and the team owners the employers. The fans were, by this logic, the customers, and as Flood noticed, the owners of baseball franchises treated fans as such, "getting as much from them as the traffic will bear and giving them no more than [they] must." In practice this meant that every decision made by the front office, especially in regard to the treatment of players, would invariably be couched in terms of being "for the good of our fans."

Unfortunately, Cardinals' owner Gussie Busch, the "most baronial" of team owners in Flood's view, exemplified this attitude and style of operation. Just before the start of the 1969 season's spring training, Busch ordered a special meeting of the entire team, including corporate executives and the press. He proceeded to blast the team for its off-season "steady diet of strike talk and dollar signs" and warned that this "has to be behind us." Of course he framed his criticisms and warnings in the name of the fans. "Fans are telling us," he proclaimed, "that if we intend to raise prices to pay for the high salaries . . . they will stop coming to the games, they will not watch, and they will not listen." It was the fans who were most concerned about the "big payrolls," and the owner of the team was putting the players on notice, although on notice of what was not entirely clear. Flood noted that "in no other industry of the Western world could an employer publicly belittle his professional staff without mass resignations." If Busch had convinced himself that his lecture would motivate his players in a positive way, he was certainly mistaken. According to Flood, the team had been "reminded that we had fewer reasons for professional pride than we had deluded ourselves into thinking." It was a message they would carry for the rest of the year. The Cardinals in 1969 were a "demoralized" team composed of "morose and touchy" players "in

{ *Chapter 2* }

a constant state of terrified insecurity." They finished in fourth place, well behind the "upstart" New York Mets.

For Flood the Busch speech was nothing short of offensive, but at the same time it was only one of a number of signs portending the center fielder's own uncertain future with the Cardinals team. "Times," he would write, "had changed," and he well understood that for a professional ballplayer, the path to and from stardom and being the favorite of team owners and management was treacherous at best. Where Flood's artistic endeavors had once been widely and enthusiastically publicized and praised as evidence of his well-rounded talents and versatility, these same accomplishments were now "deplored" as harmful distractions. Players such as Flood who attempted to develop their interests in off-season careers and businesses, mainly to prepare for the day when they would no longer be able to play baseball, were no longer viewed as prudent, responsible adults and family men but as "greedy" and not dedicated. Flood's failure to attend the preseason team banquet, described in the previous chapter, was another sign, as was his protest during a crucial time that season when Manager Red Schoendienst changed the line-up in a way that placed several younger, less experienced hitters in the middle of the batting order. When Flood's protest was made public, Cardinals' management blamed the complaint on team veterans "afraid of losing their jobs." What in previous seasons would have been viewed as evidence of his experienced leadership and intense desire for his team to win now was interpreted as the disgruntled whine of an overpaid veteran of questionable usefulness to a team whose strategy would now focus on "rebuilding" with younger players.

As if all this were not enough, it was evident that his life off the field was becoming increasingly unsettled. He divorced, remarried, and divorced a second time his wife, Beverly. "Those were hard days, baby," he would write. "You try to leave your domestic troubles at home and do your thing in front of 40,000 people, and your mind wanders to the bitterness and guilt." Then in late 1966 Johnny Jorgensen was found brutally murdered in the engraving plant in which he and Flood were partners. Although Johnny's murderer was eventually caught, it did not help that both Flood and Johnny's wife, Marian, were taken into custody by the police, questioned, and given lie-detector tests. Eventually Flood would convince Marian, "Babe," to move to St. Louis, where she "took command" of his household, his business, and his "scandalous" lifestyle. But her impact did not extend to Flood alone. It was Marian who helped Flood's troubled and brilliant older brother Carl get paroled from a federal prison. Afterward, when Carl moved to St. Louis to work in Curt's business, it was Marian who tried to get Carl over his morphine addiction. And it was Marian who continued to support and help Carl after his arrest during a bungled jewelry-store robbery in 1969, despite Curt's response of wanting to "shut him out" of his life. Curt Flood characterized Marian as "my partner and my friend," but it seems clear that that description does not do justice to the depth of support she provided him, especially after his trade. It was no surprise, at least to those who knew her and understood their relationship, that he dedicated his book to her and to the memory of her husband.

Thus, when Curt Flood and his team of lawyers entered the federal courthouse in New York City in May 1970 to begin his trial challenging baseball's reserve clause, it must have seemed like a uniquely historical moment. Here was a professional ballplayer, dressed not in a numbered uniform of cardinal-red and white but in a dark business suit and tie, entering a field of battle far different from the one he had known and competed on so successfully since childhood. In fact, it is likely that by this time Flood and certainly his attorneys, if not the public, were aware that this was by no means the first time a ballplayer had traded in his pinstripes, glove, and cleats for the more conventional courtroom attire of suit and tie. And it was by no means the first time that a baseball player had used the courtroom and the legal system to attempt to obtain redress for a grievance against the individuals who owned and ran professional leagues and teams. The issues that Flood would raise touched on fundamental concerns about the status and role of the professional player that were as old as professional baseball itself. Indeed, part of the transformation of the game of baseball into a large-scale corporate enterprise revealed itself in earlier legal battles. Judge Irving Cooper may have thought of the trial as the start of the "second inning" of the game, but if that was how the participants wanted to look at it, the game was part of a series of contests that stretched back almost a century.

CHAPTER 3

"Just a Game"

Exact beginnings are often a tricky matter for historians to pin down, and that certainly holds true for those who would trace the origins of the game of baseball. The search to find out exactly when, and where, baseball was born has resulted in an exponentially expanding body of books, articles, and, more recently, documentary films. Likewise, the many other strands that make up the narrative of sports and baseball history in America have been researched and presented in all their remarkable variety and detail, from the history of the Negro Leagues to the evolution of the ballpark. Although Curt Flood's legal challenge to baseball touched many of these different strands, it was the history of the relationship between the players, the owners of the teams for which they played, and the law that mattered most to the center fielder once he entered the courtroom in May 1970. Flood's lawsuit was by no means the first time a baseball player had traded his uniform and equipment for a suit and briefcase in order to compete on a different "field of dreams." So to answer the question of "when," it is arguable that the part of baseball history that mattered most to Curt Flood had its beginning in the year 1890. It was in that year that two events took place, one in a New York courtroom and the other in the U.S. Congress, that would shape the relationship between bench, bar, and ball field for the next eighty years.

By 1890 what had started as a gentlemanly game played by amateurs in fields and parks around the country had become organized and its players paid professionals. This initial transformation clearly reflected the entrepreneurial spirit of late-nineteenth-century America, exemplified in the "rags to riches" success of men such as Andrew Carnegie, John D. Rockefeller, and J. P. Morgan. Harry Wright, a player himself, put together the first professional team in 1869. His team, the Cincinnati Red Stockings, proved that people would pay to see what had previously been free, if the quality of play justified it—which in turn became possible if the players were paid. Within a decade, the number of these professional teams had multiplied, but without any overall organization or structure, schedules and competition were chaotic and players regularly moved from team to team depending on the salary offered. To end this period of what economists would have described as "cutthroat competition," the National League was formed in 1876. It set up regular schedules, allocated specific territories to participating teams and franchises, and allowed teams to charge a uniform ticket price of 50 cents. In order to deal with the problem of "revolving players," the league in 1879 created what would become known as the "reserve system." Under this arrangement, each team could "reserve" five players, in effect preventing those players from negotiating with other teams. Each team in the league was bound not to negotiate with the players so reserved. What started out with only five players had increased by 1890 so that the entire rosters of the league's teams had to agree to the "reserve clause" that was inserted into their annual players' contracts.

Ending the wholesale movement of players between teams may have been the prime goal of the "reserve clause," but it was clearly not the only one. Pioneer baseball historian Harold Seymour devoted an entire chapter to the clause in his history of the early years of baseball, cataloging the various other intended—and unintended—consequences of the system. Not only did the clause make it easier for owners to retain players, it also enabled them to discipline those who proved unruly or unreliable and, when necessary, to get rid of them. Indeed, the clause was referred to as the "reserve *and* release" provision. But the most important consequence of the system was that it placed the team owners in a much-strengthened position in regard to players' salaries and was an obvious way to keep those salaries low. During the 1880s this was exactly what the owners did, even while bemoaning the system. As Albert Goodwill Spaulding (A. G., as he was widely known), a former player and National League president after 1882, put it, "Professional baseball is on the wane. Salaries must come down or the interest of the public must be increased in some way." If salaries were not reduced, Spaulding predicted, the inevitable result would be "bankruptcy" and the end of professional baseball.

In 1890 one of the first legal cases involving organized baseball and its players was decided in the New York Supreme Court. John Montgomery "Monte" Ward was one of the early star professional players with Providence and then the National League's Giants. Coincidentally, and prophetically, he was also a graduate of the Columbia Law School. Five years earlier, in 1885, Ward and several of his teammates had formed what would be the first association of players, the National Brotherhood of Professional Baseball Players. Like other newly emerging labor organizations of the time, the brotherhood attempted to combat the growing power of employers through collective action. In response, baseball owners merely got tougher, introducing what became known as the "Brush classification system." This system enabled owners to "grade" players and set salary ranges for each of the five grades. It also provided for a standardized contract, which all players had to sign and which gave owners the right to renew the contracts and "assign" any player's contract to another team.

Ward and the brotherhood's reaction was to issue a "manifesto" and begin formation of their own league, the Players League. In language echoed eighty years later, the manifesto proclaimed that "players have been bought, sold, and exchanged as though they were sheep, instead of American citizens." The new league proved wildly popular with the players, who, in legal scholar Roger I. Abrams's colorful phrase, "jumped to the new league like kids in a country pond." Not surprisingly, the National League owners fought back. The Metropolitan Exhibition Company, the holder of the Giants franchise, brought suit against Monte Ward in New York state court. The lawsuit asked the court to "enjoin" Ward from playing in the new league based on his April 1889 contract with the Giants, under which he was obligated "to engage in the exhibition of the game of base ball for the said club for the period of seven months between April 1, 1889, and October 31, 1889." The plaintiff's suit also cited the provision in that contract that gave the Giants the right "to reserve the defendant for the season of 1890."

In January 1890 the New York Supreme Court ruled in the case *Metropolitan Exhibition Company v. Ward.* The opinion, written by Justice Morgan J. O'Brien, focused on two issues: the meaning and scope of the term "reserve" in the contract and whether the court could issue an injunction — or court order — in this type of case involving a contract for personal service. The court dealt with the first issue in a single paragraph. Justice O'Brien rejected Ward's contention that being "reserved" by the Giants team applied only to other teams in the National League and did not include teams *outside* that league. The second, and related, issue was whether or not Ward's contract with the Giants, reserving his future services with that team, was enforceable by a court order. This issue proved thornier for Justice O'Brien. He agreed that the contract was indeed one for "personal services" and compared a ballplayer to a professional actor: "Each is sought for his particular and peculiar fitness; each performs in public for compensation, and each possess[es] for the manager a means of attracting an audience." If either refused "to perform according to the contract," the legal remedy of an injunction would be appropriate to prevent a "loss" to the manager, especially when "such services are rendered to a rival."

The problem then for the court was to determine whether the "reserve" parts of Ward's 1889 agreement with the Giants constituted an enforceable contract. According to Justice O'Brien it did not, since it lacked specific "terms and conditions" as to what Ward had agreed to do in 1890 and the salary that he would be paid for these unspecified services. "I do not think," the justice wrote, "that Ward agrees to do anything further than to accord the right to reserve him upon terms thereafter to be fixed." The court also noted that the agreement allowed the club to terminate the players' employment at any time with ten days' notice; thus, "we have the spectacle presented of a contract which binds one party for a series of years, and the other party for ten days." Citing this "want of fairness and mutuality," the New York court refused to grant the preliminary injunction sought by the Giants, at least prior to a trial on the issues. In March 1890, after a trial, the plaintiff's complaint was dismissed "with costs." In a similar suit brought by the New York club against another defecting player, *Metropolitan Exhibition Co. v. Ewing*, a New York circuit court reached the same conclusion: The reserve clause was "merely a contract to make a contract if the parties agree." The defendant player's refusal to negotiate for the coming season was a breach of contract, but not one "the plaintiff can enforce."

Losing in the courts did not deter Spaulding and the National League from mounting a vigorous counterattack on the fledgling league. In what would become known as the "Brotherhood War," Spaulding himself headed up a "war committee" of owners and officials. They proceeded to use the superior financial resources of the National League to force the rebellious players, whom Spaulding referred to as "hotheaded anarchists," back to the league. The key to Spaulding's strategy was his unabashed support for the reserve rule and his willingness to invoke it by threatening to blacklist any player who attempted to defect to the new league. At the same time, he put pressure on the financial backers of the Players League teams by scheduling games at the same time, cutting ticket prices, and using the press to undermine the upstart league and "drive a wedge" between the players and their employers. These tactics worked, and within a year Spaulding had managed to obtain the "unconditional surrender" of the owners; eventually almost all of the defecting players returned to the National League.

The same year that the courts were dealing professional baseball its first important legal defeats, the U.S. Congress passed one of its most significant pieces of legislation, the Sherman Antitrust Act. The Sherman Act reflected hostile public reaction to the growth of giant industrial business monopolies in post–Civil War America. This hostility was directed not so much against corporations in general or the idea of incorporation but "more particularly against certain practices — above all, economic abuses — that were attributed to some corporations" such as Standard Oil or the "Sugar Trust." The act, named for Ohio Republican senator John Sherman more out of courtesy than because of actual authorship, was noticeably brief and even more noticeably vague. Section 1 (of eight) of the act made illegal "every contract, combination in the form of trust or otherwise, or conspiracy, in restraint of trade," and Section 2 made it illegal to "monopolize or attempt to monopolize, or combine to conspire . . . to monopolize any part of the trade or commerce among the several states." Another provision of the act, one that would be part of Curt Flood's lawsuit years later, allowed any person injured by the illegal actions described above to sue and "recover threefold the damages by him sustained." According to William Letwin and other legal scholars, the Sherman Act was less a compromise than a melding of the viewpoints of two late-nineteenth-century groups: economists and attorneys. Economists saw business competition and combination as necessary and inevitable. Lawyers reached back to the principles of the English common law, which "permitted combination in some instances and prohibited it in others." The result, Letwin concluded, was "a statute which by the use of common-law principles would eliminate excesses but allow 'healthy' competition and combination to flourish side by side." What exactly constituted impermissible "restraints on trade" was left to future attorneys general; the recently created Justice Department, charged with bringing prosecutions under the act; and the federal courts to work out. It seems fair to say, however, that professional baseball as of 1890 was not remotely on the minds or in the sights of the politicians and framers of the Sherman Act. Until the 1920s, the major prosecutions and interpretive Supreme Court decisions on antitrust issues involved industries and businesses far more crucial to the emergence of the United States as a world-class economic power.

Therefore, in the years following the passage of the Sherman Act, possible antitrust prosecution was not of immediate concern to baseball owners and their players, even as organized baseball in the 1890s took on the appearance of what historian Robert F. Burk labeled "monopoly ball." Having defeated the nascent Players League, Spaulding and the National League owners formalized and strengthened their control over the sport, especially the treatment of players. In 1891 they established what was called the "National Agreement," creating an owner-controlled national board with the power to review and energetically enforce league rules and contracts.

Struggles over the reserve clause and the treatment of players continued to play out in the courtroom. As in Monte Ward's case, almost all the decisions were in favor of the players, even though, as Burk concluded, they generally proved to be "Pyrrhic victories." One of the more notable of these cases involved another early star of the diamond, the second baseman for the Philadelphia Phillies, Napoleon "Nap" Lajoie. Lajoie ended up in court in much the same way that Ward had earlier, by agreeing to play for a new club, the Philadelphia Athletics. The Athletics had been created as part of a new rival professional baseball association, the American League. Organized by former Cincinnati sports reporter Ban Johnson, the new league aimed to capitalize on declining attendance at National League games during the later part of the 1890s and the dissatisfaction of many of that league's players, exemplified by the Players' Protective Association, another abortive attempt to organize.

The strategy employed by the new league's team owners, including the Athletics' Connie Mack, was to raid their rival league's team rosters by offering higher salaries to the best players. At the end of the 1900 season, the Athletics offered Lajoie $24,000 over a three-year period. After rejecting a counteroffer from the Phillies, which was actually higher than that of the Athletics, Lajoie agreed to begin playing for the new American League club in the 1901 season. But the Phillies' willingness to exceed the other team's offer suggested they were more concerned about losing their star player's services than about any immediate financial loss. So the Phillies brought suit in the Pennsylvania state court asking for an injunction, or court order, requiring Lajoie to fulfill his contractual obligation not to play for another ball club.

In *Philadelphia Ball Club, Ltd. v. Lajoie*, the Pennsylvania Supreme Court reversed the lower trial court's ruling not to grant the Phillies the injunctive relief. Unlike the court in the earlier *Ward* case, the Pennsylvania court found that Lajoie's contract with the Phillies did possess the requisite "mutuality." The defendant had agreed to "furnish his skilled professional services" to the plaintiff, in exchange for which he would be paid a salary of $2,400 (the "cap" imposed at that time by the National League). In addition, the defendant had agreed that the club could extend such services for three years by "proper notice" to the player before the end of each season. The plaintiff club retained the right to terminate the player's contract upon ten days' notice and payment of salary for the time worked and expenses for the player to get home. For the court, the fact that the preponderance of rights in the agreement favored the ball club was not enough to "destroy" that mutuality. Freedom of contract, the court concluded, did not imply an equality of rights and obligations between the parties, only that the "bounds of reasonableness and fairness are not transgressed."

Having determined that there was in fact a contract, state Supreme Court Justice William P. Potter turned his attention to the trial court's refusal to grant the injunction forcing Lajoie to play for the Phillies. For Justice Potter the key issue was whether the defendant's services were "unique, extraordinary, and of such a character as to render it impossible to replace him; so that his breach of contract would result in irreparable loss to the plaintiff." In determining that Lajoie was not irreplaceable, the trial court had relied on the famous 1852 English case of *Lumley v. Wagner*, which involved the attempt by Her Majesty's Theatre in London to prevent operatic star Johanna Wagner from singing with the rival Royal Italian Opera after she had contracted to perform for the London theater. The plaintiff argued that Wagner's "personal services" — that is, her singing — were of such a "unique" character as to be irreplaceable, but the English court refused to issue an injunction requiring the "specific performance" of her contractual obligations, although she would be financially liable for her nonper-formance. Wagner had also agreed to what the court termed a "nega-tive covenant," in which she had promised *not* to sing for any opera in the same geographic area. This provision the court was willing to enforce.

The Pennsylvania Supreme Court found that Nap Lajoie's skills were "unique" in the same way that Johanna Wagner's operatic talents had been. He was, the court said, "well known" with a "great reputa-tion"; his playing "is peculiarly meritorious as an integral part of the team work which is so essential." "He may not be the sun in the base-ball firmament," Justice Potter observed, "but he is certainly a bright particular star." It remained for the court to decide what to do about this uniqueness. Citing a rule of equity law, the court allowed that the "negative remedy of an injunction will do substantial justice between the parties" by "obliging" the defendant to carry out his contractual obligations or "lose all benefit of the breach." "The court cannot com-pel the defendant to play for the plaintiff, but it can restrain him from playing for another club in violation of his agreement." Napoleon Lajoie never again played for the Philadelphia Phillies. Prohibited by the courts from playing for the Athletics, he was traded to the new American League franchise in Cleveland. An Ohio state court later rejected the Phillies' attempt to get the Pennsylvania injunction extended to Ohio. Lajoie finished his career playing for Cleveland (whenever Cleveland had to travel to Philadelphia to play the Athlet-ics, he went on vacation to New Jersey). The Lajoie case became a landmark ruling in the evolution of baseball and sports law, in much the same way that the *Wagner* ruling would for entertainment and its evolution into an "industry." Both established the principle that in employment contracts for "personal services" with such profession-als as an opera singer or a baseball player, there was a presumption that such services were unique and irreplaceable. Although the courts could not force someone to play for a particular team or sing on a particular stage, they were willing to prevent that person from selling their services elsewhere.

In this respect the *Ward* and *Lajoie* cases were clearly reflective of the general state of that branch of law involving the making and enforcement of contracts. According to Lawrence Friedman's magisterial *A History of American Law*, the nineteenth century was, at least in theory, the "century of contract." The idea of people organizing their social and economic relationships through "free voluntary agreement" was central to American legal and constitutional thought, to the extent that this notion had even been enshrined in the Constitution with Article I, Section 10 explicitly prohibiting the states from "impairing the obligation of contracts." Yet after 1850 the law of contracts had begun what Friedman characterized as a "long slide into triviality." The sheer numbers and variety of new types of businesses and new forms of employment relationships that appeared in America simply overwhelmed the courts. Judges had been, and continued to be, trained exclusively in the law, not in business or economics, and "certainly not in the business details and jargon of a thousand fields." The legal doctrines were well settled: It was their application to novel enterprises that proved problematic. How was it possible for a judge such as Pennsylvania's Justice Potter to determine with any certainty the uniqueness of a baseball player such as Nap Lajoie? Moreover, these mainly state court judges in contract law cases did not see themselves in the role of mediators, working out compromises between competing claims. Their function was to decide "winners and losers," irrespective of the broader economic consequences.

The result was that even as individual players such as Ward and Lajoie succeeded in courtroom contests in exercising their "freedom of contract," seeking higher salaries by switching teams, professional baseball players collectively continued to suffer at the hands of owners. Then in 1903 the team owners of the National League and its more successful rival, the upstart American League, came to a "truce" by signing a new National Agreement. It seems likely that the National League owners were motivated by their courtroom defeats to try to prevent the "plundering" of their player rosters by American League owners. Like its 1891 predecessor, the National Agreement was an attempt to bring order and stability to an increasingly complex and potentially lucrative enterprise. The document created a national commission, a governing body that had almost unlimited authority to make and enforce policies and rules and adjudicate disputes, including those between players and owners. With no sense of irony, A. G. Spaulding would describe the commission as the "Supreme Court of Base Ball." The agreement also set forth a series of standardized provisions that formalized the reserve system as the basis for all of organized baseball.

The creation of the National Agreement and the merger of the American and National Leagues coincided with the ascension of Vice President Theodore Roosevelt to the presidency following the assassination of President William McKinley. It also marked the beginning of what would be called the Progressive reform era. One of the themes of Progressivism was a commitment to greater federal government regulation of business corporations. Such regulation was seen as a necessary response to an increasingly complex economy in which too much competition was seen, often by businessmen themselves, as being neither economically profitable nor efficient. The creation of organized baseball and the merger of the American and National Leagues was a unique but not atypical example of what historian Robert Wiebe characterized as early-twentieth-century America's "search for order"; baseball magnates, using the law and their own rule-making authority, sought to achieve the kind of economic stability that many other corporate enterprises were attempting through a variety of combinations and mergers. At the same time, Progressive reformers, especially the new president, were more than willing to use government authority to rein in the more visible excesses of corporate and business behavior.

One tool at hand, which had hardly been used in the decade since its passage, was the Sherman Antitrust Act. In his first message to Congress on December 3, 1901, President Roosevelt talked at length of the "real and grave evils" of corporate trusts in America and his willingness to use the "big stick" of federal authority to control and regulate abuses by these trusts and their "features and tendencies hurtful to the general welfare." Given this attitude, which Roosevelt was convinced reflected public opinion at the time, it was likely that at some point the activities of organized baseball, with its commission and growing control over professional baseball, would fall under the scrutiny of the "trust-busters." As had been happening in other businesses, it was the appearance of new competitors that opened up the issue of baseball and monopoly. In 1914 a new league emerged to challenge the dominance of the Major Leagues. The Federal League, as it was called, was organized in various unique ways: instead of individually owned franchises, clubs were run collectively by the league; new players were to be given signing bonuses; and veteran players were guaranteed regular raises. Most unusual was an early form of what would come to be called free agency: the provision that after ten years, players would be free to find another club to play for if they chose. Like its predecessors, the Federal League intended to staff its rosters with defecting players from the established American and National Leagues.

One player whom the Federal League managed to entice from the majors was Harold "Hal" Chase of the American League's Chicago White Sox. In 1914, Chase, described as "the foremost first baseman in professional baseball," had signed the standard player's contract with the Sox, as prescribed by the National Agreement. In June of that year Chase notified the team of his intent to "avoid, cancel and annul the agreement" and shortly thereafter signed with the Buffalo Buf-Feds club of the upstart Federal League. White Sox officials thereupon sought and obtained a temporary injunction in New York prohibiting Chase from playing with the new club. In July 1914 New York Supreme Court Judge Herbert P. Bissell, in *The American League Baseball Club of Chicago v. Harold H. Chase*, reversed the lower court's ruling. Interestingly, Judge Bissell had run unsuccessfully the previous year for mayor of Buffalo as a pro–business development Democrat. The judge's ruling began by examining the same issues presented in the earlier court rulings: contract law, specific performance, and equity jurisprudence. However, the court not only looked at the contract between Chase and the White Sox but also included a "somewhat extended analysis" of the relevant provisions of the National Agreement and the rules of the national commission. Citing a number of precedents, including *Lajoie*, the New York court decided that the standard player's contract promulgated by the agreement lacked the "mutuality" necessary for an enforceable contract. Moreover, the court reiterated the proposition from those rulings that injunctions could not be used to enforce negative provisions of a contract, that is, a player's inability to play for another team.

At this point the *Chase* decision appeared little different from the other state court cases involving professional baseball players' contracts and attempts by team owners to control where and under what conditions their players played. But Judge Bissell went on to deal with another, new issue "presented with much earnestness" by Chase's attorneys. That issue was whether the National Agreement "and the rules and regulations adopted pursuant thereof" violated the Sherman Antitrust Act. This seems to be the first time that a court on any level faced this question, and in response Judge Bissell made two important points. He acknowledged that the "game of baseball" had become something more than that, although his account of the game's origins as an "athletic sport of youthful players attending the schools and colleges throughout the country" was rather fanciful. Baseball, however, had become "commercialized and organized," and although the game remained the "favorite athletic sport of America," organized baseball had "developed into a big business conducted for profit." Baseball was no longer just a game, or even just a "business," as it had been characterized in Nap Lajoie's case. It was now a "big business."

But whether "Organized Baseball," as the court referred to the American and National Leagues and the National Agreement, was not just a big business but a monopoly prohibited by the Sherman Act proved more problematic. Organized Baseball, Judge Bissell concluded, was most certainly a monopoly, one "ingeniously devised and created in so far as a monopoly can be created among free men." But it was *not* a monopoly insofar as the antitrust laws were concerned because the "business of baseball" was not in "interstate trade or commerce." This may seem to have been a remarkable, if not absurd, conclusion. Baseball was a business with teams located in different cities and states. In order to engage in their particular "business," players had to travel to those different cities and across state lines. Moreover, the products and equipment used by the players, such as uniforms, bats, balls, and gloves, came from other states, as did the food, beverage, and souvenir items sold to fans attending the games. How then could baseball not be interstate commerce?

In determining that baseball was not interstate commerce, the New York court relied on the U.S. Supreme Court's landmark 1895 opinion in the *E. C. Knight* case. In that decision, one of the first to involve the interpretation and meaning of the Sherman Act, the Supreme Court determined that the manufacture and processing of sugar (the case involved the so-called Sugar Trust) did not constitute interstate commerce for purposes of the act because the manufacturing took place "within" the boundaries of a state. Commerce or trade involved actual goods or commodities, and interstate commerce meant the movement of these across state lines. That manufactured products were then shipped to another state, or that making them required items coming from other states, was incidental and only an "indirect" aspect of commerce. The Sherman Act, the Court decided, contemplated only "direct" effects on limiting commerce. This judicial distinction between direct and indirect effects would severely limit the federal government's attempts to enforce antitrust statutes until the 1930s. Baseball, Judge Bissell now proclaimed, was "an amusement, a sport, a game," and one that clearly came "within the civil and criminal law of the state . . . and it is not a commodity or an article of merchandise subject to the regulation of congress on the theory that it is interstate commerce."

In 1914 in the New York courts, the distinction between indirect and direct effects on commerce appeared to be a distinction that made a difference. Or did it? Since the court had not been asked to dissolve the monopoly, even if it had been found "illegal," why did Judge Bissell even address the issue? Because, the judge argued, it was relevant to the question of the injunctions and equity law. Citing another common-law notion that parties to an equity law case must come to the court "with clean hands," Judge Bissell used baseball's monopoly status as part of his argument that organized baseball did not have the requisite "clean hands" and therefore was not entitled to an injunction to prevent Chase from jumping leagues. But Judge Bissell did not stop there. Raising an issue that Curt Flood would resurrect in 1970, Judge Bissell concluded that the National Agreement established "a species of *quasi*-peonage unlawfully controlling and interfering with the personal freedom of the men employed," "one that was "contrary" to both the spirit of "American institutions" and the Constitution. The National Agreement "reveals the involuntary character of the servitude which is imposed upon the players by the strength of the combination controlling the labor of practically all of the players in the country." Given all this, the New York court justified its reversal of the lower court's injunction because not to do so would be tantamount to assisting an agreement that had as its purpose the creation of not only a monopoly but one that interfered with the "personal liberty of a citizen" and the right of any citizen to control his "free right to labor wherever and for whom he pleases."

As a practical matter, the *Chase* decision, like earlier cases, had little impact on the individual players and teams who sought judicial redress for their grievances. Whether courts ruled in favor of players or against them, such victories tended to be, as noted earlier, "Pyrrhic victories" as the real action continued outside the courtroom. However, the upstart Federal League did find in the *Chase* ruling a possible line of attack. In 1913 the league filed suit against organized baseball in federal court in Illinois. The suit alleged specifically that organized baseball — the American and National Leagues — was a violation of the Sherman Antitrust Act. In yet another historical irony, the case was brought before Judge Kenesaw Mountain Landis, who would later become the new commissioner of the Major Leagues in the wake of the 1919 "Black Sox" scandal. Although Judge Landis was known as sympathetic to Progressive trust-busting, it was evident that he was wary of putting baseball in the same category as big oil or big steel. While taking the case "under advisement" for almost a year Landis urged both sides to reach some sort of settlement. In fact, in December 1915 a "peace agreement" between the leagues was reached by way of most of the Federal League's more successful franchises being incorporated into the Major Leagues.

One of the franchises excluded from the new expanded Major Leagues was the Baltimore Terrapins (it is likely they were excluded because they simply did not bother to show up during the negotiations). The Terrapins' owners then brought suit against organized baseball in March 1916, although the suit was dropped three months later pending a possible out-of-court settlement. When those negotiations broke down, the suit was refiled later that year in federal district court in Washington, D.C. However, *Federal Baseball Club of Baltimore v. National League of Professional Baseball, et al.*, was not tried until 1919. The Baltimore plaintiffs based their suit on much the same arguments that had been put forth by Hal Chase's attorneys five years earlier. Organized baseball was a monopoly in interstate commerce and therefore a violation of the Sherman Antitrust Act. The National Agreement, especially the reserve clause and its attendant provisions, enabled the National and American Leagues (and the "minor league" franchises that were also a party to the agreement) to "monopolize the base ball business." It was alleged that organized baseball had used this power to destroy the Federal League by buying up some of the League clubs "and in one way or another inducing all those clubs except the plaintiff to leave their league," thus causing "great damage" to the plaintiffs.

The trial judge, Wendell P. Stafford, agreed with the plaintiffs, ruling that the exhibition of baseball games did constitute interstate "trade and commerce" and that organized baseball had acted in a monopolistic fashion in ways prohibited by the Sherman Act. The jury determined that the amount of damages to be awarded Baltimore was $80,000, which Judge Stafford increased to $240,000 under the "treble damages" provisions of the Sherman Act. Organized baseball immediately appealed the ruling, and in December 1920 Chief Justice Constantine J. Smyth of the District of Columbia Circuit Court reversed the district court's decision. Following Judge Bissell's reasoning in the *Chase* case, Justice Smyth concluded that baseball was not a form of interstate commerce and therefore was not subject to congressional regulation. Commerce, he wrote, requires the transfer "of something, whether it be persons, commodities, or intelligence, from one place or person to another." A baseball game is an "exhibition," and even though players and their equipment travel from place to place in interstate commerce, "they are not the game." Since both the Federal League and the Major Leagues were "organized" for the same purpose, that is, the exhibition of these baseball games, the Major Leagues could not be considered an "interference" with "interstate trade or commerce" as prohibited by the Sherman Act.

But then the chief justice departed from the earlier *Chase* decision in a very significant way. Whereas Judge Bissell had had no problem viewing organized baseball as a business and the National Agreement as an example of a monopoly, albeit an intrastate one, Chief Justice Smyth ruled that organized baseball was neither a business nor a monopoly. It was a "sport," and the fact that the games were played "as a source of profit, large or small, cannot change the character of the games. They are still sport, not trade." Whereas the New York judge had described the reserve system as a form of "peonage" amounting to almost "involuntary servitude," Justice Smyth found the system merely "incidental" to the general purpose of the baseball enterprise. Indeed, the chief justice defended the system, calling it a "reasonable" method on the part of the Major Leagues to preserve the "competitive balance" among the teams. Without the reserve system, "the highly skillful players would be absorbed by the more wealthy clubs, and thus some clubs in the league would so far outstrip others in playing ability that the contests . . . would be uninteresting, and the public would refuse to patronize them." The reserve system deterred "contract jumping" and punished those players who did so by using a form of "blacklisting" to prevent other teams from hiring them.

An appeal of the District of Columbia court's ruling was argued before the U.S. Supreme Court on April 19, 1922. A month later a unanimous Supreme Court ruling, authored by Justice Oliver W. Holmes Jr., affirmed Justice Smyth's ruling. The Court's opinion was remarkably brief — five paragraphs in all — and the first three mainly restated the basic facts and issues of the case as presented by the Court of Appeals. According to Justice Holmes, the circuit court had gotten to the "root of the case" and was "correct" in determining that the business of baseball consisted of giving "exhibitions," which as such "are purely state affairs." Using the same reasoning, and even citing the same illustrations as the lower court, the Supreme Court decided that organized baseball was not in interstate trade or commerce, and therefore the "restrictions by contract," that is, the reserve system, and "other conduct" to prevent players from joining other teams was "not an interference" in such commerce.

Given what would become its precedent-setting and "landmark" status for the rest of the century, the Supreme Court's ruling in *Federal Baseball* was an example of judicial decision-making that became both more and less than it actually was; as the scholar Paul Finkelman would note, it was a ruling "often discussed, but seldom read." The decision was responsible for creating the "baseball anomaly," or, as it became commonly referred to, baseball's "exemption" from the Sherman Antitrust Act. Yet neither the Sherman Act nor any mention of "antitrust" or "monopoly" appeared in Holmes's opinion. This ruling became the precedent that Curt Flood's attorneys would confront in

1971 in challenging the reserve system, yet that system itself was alluded to only once by the phrase "restrictions by contract," and then in a single elliptical sentence at the end of the opinion. If, as Justice Holmes himself wrote in an earlier antitrust ruling, "great cases like hard cases make bad law," then it may well be asked what made this case "great" because many commentators then and since have agreed on how "bad" it was.

Since 1922 the Supreme Court's ruling in *Federal Baseball* has been extensively analyzed in articles and books. Much like the game the ruling purported to judge, such commentary has in the main focused on choosing sides, whether or not the writer thought the decision a good or, far more commonly, a bad or erroneous decision. Just about every aspect of the ruling has been analyzed, including the Court's and especially Justice Holmes's familiarity with baseball. The conclusions run the gamut from Holmes being a good ballplayer himself to the likelihood that he had never witnessed a professional baseball game in his life. In fairness, it should be noted that at least one justice on the Supreme Court at the time, newly appointed chief justice and former U.S. president William H. Taft, had in 1909 become the first president to witness a professional ball game and a year later had started the tradition of presidents throwing out the first ceremonial pitch of the Major League season. Taft was quoted as saying that he "liked the game," especially when there was lots of "slugging."

It is necessary to understand the decision in its historical context, in terms of both the era's overall concern with economic issues and business regulation and the position of organized baseball as it was then operating. Jerrold J. Duquette, in his exhaustive study of baseball and antitrust, persuasively argued that granting baseball's monopoly exemption was "wholly consistent with the spirit and substantive goals" of Progressivism. Progressive reformers believed that some business combinations were necessary as long as they were "consistent with the public good or national interest." Baseball became in that sense "anomalous" precisely because it was the "only industry of its size and scope that was not subjected to regulation by the federal government." Similarly, legal historian and Holmes scholar G. Edward White explained the Supreme Court's "astonishing inability" to recognize baseball as a business monopoly as another "example of the 'peculiar' status of baseball as an American enterprise." The Supreme Court, like most Americans at the time, resisted the notion that professional baseball in reality had indeed become more than just a "child's game, played for the pure joy of outdoor activity and competition." The Supreme Court had also managed to resist a substantial body of case law, admittedly from state courts, such as the Nap Lajoie and Hal Chase decisions, which unequivocally treated baseball as the business it had become.

It can also be argued that by 1922 the Progressive reform impulse had largely run its course, sped along by America's participation in World War I. Recently elected Republican president Warren G. Harding's idea of returning the postwar nation to "normalcy" did not include active government regulation of economic matters, especially when it came to trusts and monopolies. Indeed, the 1920s would witness one of the largest number of mergers and combinations since the Sherman Act had become law. Nor did government policy, as is commonly believed, reflect a return to the extreme Social Darwinian laissez-faire doctrines of the past. Rather, the emphasis shifted to a less-acknowledged strain of Progressive ideology—business self-regulation and business-government cooperation. Presidents Roosevelt and Wilson had exemplified this notion in one way by staffing newly created government regulatory agencies such as the Bureau of Corporations and the Federal Trade Commission with former business executives, "experts" with ties to those industries they were appointed to regulate. A variation of this idea in the 1920s was the prolific growth of "trade associations," organized bodies of businesses and industries engaged in similar enterprises that formulated and enforced rules and policies that promoted the best interests of that particular industry. From the point of view of 1920s economic policy, organized baseball's commission system was exactly what was needed to solidify the organization's legal standing and ensure the future economic growth of the game.

At the time that the Supreme Court announced its decision in the *Federal Baseball* case, professional baseball was just emerging from one of its most infamous and defining moments, the so-called Black Sox scandal, in which members of the Chicago White Sox team were accused of throwing the 1919 World Series to Cincinnati. One of the consequences of the scandal was that baseball reorganized itself yet again, creating a new position, the commissioner, who was given broad and unquestioned authority over the teams and their players. As mentioned before, the person appointed to that position, with a mandate to "clean up" baseball, was Judge Kenesaw M. Landis, the federal jurist before whom the case had originally been heard.

More than Just a Game

In the years following the Supreme Court's *Federal Baseball* ruling, professional baseball completed its "transformation" into America's national pastime. In becoming "much more than a game," professional baseball embarked on an era of remarkable growth and stability, its "golden age," as some would describe it. Like the American economy in general, organized baseball in the 1920s experienced remarkable prosperity, with soaring revenues, attendance, and profits. Thanks to such innovations as the radio and motion pictures and the development of a cadre of brilliant and enthusiastic baseball journalists and writers, baseball's visibility and popularity blossomed. America during the "roaring '20s" also witnessed another relatively new and complementary phenomenon in the form of supercelebrities. These were individuals who, thanks to the new media and the emergence of strategic marketing and advertising as exemplified by Madison Avenue, became larger-than-life figures. In baseball, the reigning celebrity was George Herman Ruth, the "Babe." His exploits on and off the field became daily fodder for millions of readers and listeners who, through the new mass media, could vicariously experience the excitement and drama of this sport with an immediacy heretofore unimaginable.

Yet, like the American economy and society in general, professional baseball in the 1920s had more than one side. For professional ballplayers themselves, the picture was not as spectacular as those who followed the exploits of a superstar such as the Babe might think. The main reason for this was Baseball Commissioner Kenesaw Mountain Landis. Judge Landis, as noted in Chapter 3, had been directed by team owners to clean up the game in the wake of the Black Sox scandal. In Landis's mind this above all else meant ridding the game of those players whose behavior on or off the field hurt the game and its image in the public imagination. Such conduct included more than just the gambling and game-fixing associated with the 1919 scandal. It also included "morals misconduct" and playing for money in pickup games during the off-season — "barnstorming," as it was called. Just as importantly, Landis was more than willing to enforce the reserve clause in cases of contract-jumping and the "raiding" of players by other teams. With the complete support of the owners, he never hesitated to blacklist "outlaw" players who tried to play either for a different team or, in the case of the various minor leagues, a different circuit.

Although he was less eager to admit it publicly, Commissioner Landis was also committed to the preservation of another important feature of organized baseball in the 1920s — the exclusion of African American players. Landis justified keeping "these ballplayers" out of the sport by comparing them to the "outlaws" who gambled, cheated, or acted in immoral ways detrimental to baseball's good name and clean image. Behind such justifications was the tragic reality that by the 1920s racism and racial segregation had become an institutionalized part of American society. Whether by Jim Crow laws or social custom, white and black Americans existed from cradle to grave in separate and unequal communities; not surprisingly, this division extended to the baseball diamond as well. But it had not always been that way. Indeed, it is fair to say that African Americans "were present in significant ways in baseball's first decades — present, indeed at the creation." Oral histories compiled by the Federal Writer's Project during the 1930s reveal that the game was known to antebellum slaves. In the years after the Civil War, baseball among African Americans developed pretty much along the same lines as it did for whites, going from "unorganized amusement" to contests between more or less organized clubs and teams, mainly in northern cities such as Philadelphia and New York. Although organized baseball among black Americans developed on a largely separate but parallel track alongside its white counterpart, in the last two decades of the nineteenth century there was some connection in the form of African American ballplayers such as John "Bud" Fowler, Moses Fleetwood Walker, and Frank Grant who played for white professional teams, mainly in the Midwest and Northeast.

By the end of the century, however, professional baseball had become, like most of America, racially segregated. In response, following the "self-help" philosophy of leaders such as the Tuskegee Institute's Booker T. Washington, African Americans began creating their own institutions and businesses. Such enterprises ran the gamut from small grocery and clothing stores to hospitals, theaters, hotels, and universities. Organized baseball was no exception, and during the first decades of the century a number of attempts were made to organize leagues of professional black baseball teams. The most successful of these efforts was Andrew "Rube" Foster's Negro National League. Foster was a former star ballplayer (he once tutored the great pitcher Christy Mathewson) who during the early 1900s became involved in booking black teams barnstorming the country. Despite his success, Foster came to realize that for black players, this type of competition was a "losing proposition," especially since the stadiums where such contests were held were white-owned, as were many of the teams. Foster also recognized that sometime in the future organized baseball would accept black players, and it was his remarkable insight that a well-organized and well-run Negro league would provide a perfect "base" for that eventuality. Aided by the Great Migration of thousands of African Americans from the rural South to northern cities in the years during and after World War I, Foster organized eight teams, including his own Chicago Black Giants, into the Negro National League in December 1920.

Negro League baseball would continue for the next three decades, even though Foster's leadership ended after six years and a new league was created in 1932. The "rise and ruin" of these attempts has been thoroughly examined in recent years. Negro League baseball both succeeded and failed because it attempted on one hand to replicate in many ways the structure and functional arrangements of organized baseball while on the other hand promoting and continuing Foster's vision of a unique, "Africanized" sports enterprise. An important example was the contractual relationship between team owners and players. In the bylaws of Foster's 1920 Negro National League, team owners agreed not to lure players from other team's rosters by offering higher salaries or other incentives. Like his Major League counterpart Judge Landis, Foster believed that such "raiding" and team-jumping was not in the "best interests" of his fledgling league; like the managers of organized baseball, he introduced a standard player contract that included a reserve clause! The clause operated in the same way as in organized baseball: Once a player signed the contract with a particular team, he was bound to that team for the following season. Related provisions allowed owners and the league commissioner to discipline or fire players who engaged in "immoral" behavior or misconduct on or off the field.

At least in theory, the Negro League's reserve system imposed the same kind of "bondage" that Curt Flood would challenge in the Major Leagues years later. An irony, certainly, yet for a variety of reasons the actual impact and enforcement of the system during the life of the Negro League was far more ambiguous than it was in organized baseball. For one thing, not all players even signed contracts, and as Neil Lanctot's history of Negro League baseball concluded, some clubs did not bother using contracts at all. Two former Negro League players who went on to integrate the Major Leagues, Jackie Robinson and Roy Campanella, apparently never signed formal contracts with the Negro League teams for which they played. In Robinson's case, a letter from Kansas City Monarchs owner Tom Baird was all the contract he "needed." Even players with signed contracts did not always take them seriously. As one former player, Bill Yancey, remembered: "They were regular contracts. But we didn't pay much attention to them. You signed up for a year. All right, you played that year, but if you felt like jumping the next year, you jumped. There was a reserve clause in it, but it was disregarded; that's the reason I played for so many clubs. If I was unhappy I said the hell with this and I jumped."

At the same time, the absence of contracts or the use of "makeshift agreements" often proved beneficial to team owners. Injured players, for example, could be released during the season and denied their promised season's salary. This would happen even if the player had a contract. In 1940 the Newark Eagles released veteran pitcher Daltie Cooper after he injured his foot in a game. The team refused to pay Cooper the balance of his season's salary, so the left-hander filed a grievance with New Jersey's Workman's Compensation Bureau. Cooper won, but his victory apparently did little to stop the practice, and he never played organized ball again.

By most accounts, players jumping from one club to another and the raiding of players by other teams was fairly common throughout the existence of the Negro League. This seemed particularly true during the Great Depression years. The scarcity of jobs outside the sport encouraged owners to get the best players for the lowest salary and players to seek the "best deals" they could, even if it meant jumping to another club at any time. In the words of the writer Robert Peterson, the situation became a "two way street," one that was self-perpetuating because so many teams and players either engaged in or tolerated such practices. A team that lost a player or players to another team could always raid other players from that same team, and in some cases owners even lent players to other teams for specific periods or even games. When the situation seemed to be getting out of hand, team owners would simply get together and informally arrange "gentlemen's agreements" designed to restore "peace" and their version of competitive stability. Yet it was an uneasy peace because it depended on players, such as Bill Yancey, ignoring their legal obligations and on players' willingness to be lured or lent to other teams. At the same time, "the owners remained content to function within an unsatisfactory system that offered little protection but occasionally allowed considerable leeway with players."

In at least one notable instance, a Negro League team did successfully use the courts to enforce its control over a player. The case involved one of the most famous and greatest players of the leagues, catcher Josh Gibson of Pittsburgh's Homestead Grays. It arose from what in the late 1930s became an external threat to the Negro League: the loss of its players to professional baseball teams south of the U.S. border, especially Mexico. After signing a contract to play for the Grays in 1941, Gibson left the country to play for a Mexican League club at twice the $3,000 salary he was to earn with the Grays. The team sued Gibson in the Allegheny County, Pennsylvania, Court of Common Pleas for breach of contract and $10,000 in damages. Citing the early-twentieth-century Pennsylvania court ruling in the Nap Lajoie case, Judge Thomas Marshall ruled in favor of the Grays, agreeing with the team's contention that its contract with Gibson had the requisite "mutuality." The court rejected Gibson's claim (made to a U.S. consul in Mexico) that he had been given permission to play in Mexico by a team official. The suit was ultimately dropped when Gibson, rather than lose his property through a seizure of his home ordered by the Pennsylvania court, agreed to return to the Grays for the 1942 season.

Given such decisions and the Supreme Court's *Federal Baseball* rul-

{ *Chapter 4* }

ing, it is a matter of speculation why owners of Negro League teams "continued to prefer less formal agreements" with the players rather than using the courts and the legal precedents that would have supported their efforts to create a stable and perhaps a more economically viable enterprise. Under the circumstances, the less formal system may simply have worked best for all involved. Jackie Robinson, who spent a short time in the Negro League, claimed that when he first entered the league as a Kansas City Monarch, he was never even offered a contract. He admitted that the reason was simple: The team managers were not sure he would make it in the league. Likewise, and perhaps even more ironically, if Negro League owners had employed a real reserve system, would there have been a player like Curt Flood willing to challenge a system that even hinted at why there were no African American players in the Major Leagues at the time?

The defection of Josh Gibson and other star Negro League players to the Mexican League beginning in the 1930s proved significant for organized baseball as well. The primary lure for African American players was of course the money, as many of the Mexican team owners were wealthy businessmen who were both eager and able to offer black players, especially proven performers such as Gibson, salaries they could only have dreamed about earning in the States. Given organized baseball's tight control over players through the reserve system, Mexican team owners avoided trying to lure Major League players. Moreover, the Depression had further solidified baseball's control over its players, since jobs were scarce and players had little choice but to accept whatever terms and conditions were offered. This situation changed dramatically at the end of World War II as thousands of American soldiers, including many professional ballplayers, returned home. Major League team owners believed that these returning players would be grateful for whatever salaries and terms were offered. What owners did not anticipate was that Mexico would start competing for the same players. The president of the Mexican League, Jorge Pasquel, was a wealthy businessman who believed he had the resources to draw sufficient numbers of Major League players to ensure the success of his enterprise.

One of the seventeen Major Leaguers lured to Mexico was Danny Gardella, an outfielder with the New York Giants. Gardella had been picked up by the Giants in 1944 while working at the New York City shipyards. During his two seasons with the team, he batted a respectable but not outstanding .250 and .272; before the 1946 season the Giants offered him a new contract but with only a $500 increase in salary. For Gardella, the message was clear: With all those returning veterans, he was now expendable and would no doubt be headed to the minor leagues if he signed the contract offered. Angry at this "shabby treatment," he "decided to take my gifted talents to Mexico." In February 1946 he signed a five-year contract to play in Mexico, frankly admitting, "They are paying me more so why shouldn't I play in Mexico?" In response, Baseball Commissioner Albert "Happy" Chandler threatened a five-year suspension for any player who left the country. For a number of reasons, not the least being hostility between native Mexican players and the much-higher-paid Americans, most of the players, including Gardella, returned after only one season. Banned from baseball, he and the others had to rely on barnstorming and odd jobs, but what they really wanted was to reenter organized baseball. So in 1948 Gardella became the first player to file a suit challenging baseball's reserve system. Three of the other defecting players also would file lawsuits, but because he had never signed his contract with the Giants, Gardella's case was considered the strongest. With his attorney, Frederic A. Johnson (who had been a law school classmate of Commissioner Chandler), Gardella claimed that the reserve clause violated the Sherman and Clayton Antitrust Acts. He asked for $100,000 in damages, which under the provisions of the Sherman Act was trebled. League attorneys moved to dismiss the case based on the *Federal Baseball* precedent, arguing that baseball was not a form of interstate commerce, and on July 14, 1948, U.S. District Court judge Henry Goddard agreed. However, on appeal a three-judge panel of the Court of Appeals for the Second Circuit reversed that ruling by a two-to-one vote and ordered that a trial be held on the merits of Gardella's case.

The Court of Appeals ruling only ordered a trial to be held for Gardella's lawsuit, but it was a remarkable decision in a number of ways. The one vote to deny a trial was cast by Judge Harrie B. Chase. Judge Chase argued that the Supreme Court's *Federal Baseball* ruling was "controlling," and no matter what the outcome of a trial might be, "our duty as a subordinate court" was to follow that ruling, which exempted baseball from the antitrust statutes. Moreover, Chase concluded that Gardella's suit had failed to even state a triable "cause of action" because even if organized baseball "controlled" the employment of its players through the reserve system, that employment and the means of earning a livelihood were "not subject" to interstate commerce and antitrust laws. For Chase, neither baseball nor the meaning of interstate commerce had changed since 1922.

The two judges who voted to allow a trial were Learned B. Hand and Jerome Frank, both among the most eminent and respected federal jurists and regularly considered as potential Supreme Court appointees. Judge Frank served as head of the Securities and Exchange Commission in the 1930s, and Judge Hand had been on the Second Circuit Court since 1924. By the 1930s the Second Circuit had even become known as the "Learned Hand Court" as a result of his intellect and leadership. Judge Hand was unwilling to agree that baseball's reserve clause itself was a violation of the Sherman Act. What he did believe was that thanks to the now regular broadcasts of baseball games on radio and television, the arrangements between the ball clubs and the outlets went beyond being "merely incidents of the business," as the Supreme Court had found to be the case with the various interstate activities associated with the game in 1922. As a result, professional baseball was now most certainly "engaged in interstate commerce." Judge Frank's opinion went even further, beginning with the remarkable statement that court decisions since 1922 had left the *Federal Baseball* case "but an impotent zombie." Like Hand, Judge Frank concluded that broadcasts of baseball contests were not simply incidental to the business but an important part of its popularity and operation. The Supreme Court in *Federal Baseball* had, in Frank's view, correctly decided that the business of "giving exhibitions" of baseball was purely a "state affair" even though it involved the "travel" of players, people, and articles across state lines. What distinguished the present case was that now "the games themselves because of the radio and television are, so to speak, played interstate as well as intrastate." Moreover, court decisions since the 1920s had expanded the definition and scope of interstate commerce such that the business of baseball fell within the scope of such commerce. Although he was "hesitant" about telling the Supreme Court it was "once wrong," Judge Frank concluded that although that Court had never explicitly "over-ruled" its decision in *Federal Baseball*, it had most certainly "over-ruled the precedents upon which that decision was based." Such a retraction, in his mind, was clearly "foreshadowed."

Judge Frank's opinion in the *Gardella* case also distinguished itself from the earlier Supreme Court ruling in another, more relevant way. Judge Frank concluded that baseball's reserve clause "results in something resembling peonage of the baseball player" and that the reserve system was a "monopoly" that "possesses characteristics shockingly repugnant to moral principles that, at least since the War Between the States, have been basic to the Constitution as shown by the Thirteenth Amendment to the Constitution." Judge Frank, citing a number of the nineteenth-century cases described in Chapter 3, conceded that the courts had often refused to enforce player contracts under the various national agreements. However, baseball had made use of "extra-legal penalties" such as "blacklisting" to ensure that ballplayers could never play for another team without their original team's consent. For ballplayers, it was a take-it-or-leave-it proposition, and Judge Frank ironically noted that a player who violated the system "may perhaps become a judge (with a less exciting and often less remunerative occupation) or a bartender, or a street-sweeper, but his chances of ever again playing baseball are exceedingly slim." Although Judge Frank conceded that the reserve system was not itself a violation of the Thirteenth Amendment, he did "suggest" that such contracts were "so opposed to the public policy of the United States" that they should be "deemed within the prohibitions of the Sherman Act."

Not unexpectedly, organized baseball reacted to the circuit court's decision with what had by now become its standard litany of fears and consequences—the end of the reserve system would benefit only a few of the wealthier players and would "ruin" baseball. One of the more interesting reactions came from Brooklyn Dodgers general manager Branch Rickey, who had recently gained notoriety and baseball immortality of his own by signing Jackie Robinson and beginning the process of integrating Major League baseball. Rickey accused Gardella and those players who supported him of "communist tendencies." Such criticism was not surprising given that this was the beginning of the Cold War years, though in Rickey's case it was ironic because he had been targeted in the same way for integrating America's national pastime. For his part, Gardella remained adamant about continuing his case and denied that he was "undermining the structure of baseball."

All he wanted was to "end a baseball evil," and he looked forward to the trial, set to begin in the fall of 1949. That June Commissioner Chandler announced an end to the suspensions of players provided that those players withdrew their lawsuits. Two of them did so and were allowed to return to baseball, but Gardella refused, and preparations for the trial went forward, including the deposition of the commissioner. Then suddenly, on October 7, 1949, Gardella announced that he was withdrawing his suit and would be playing for the St. Louis Cardinals the following season

Although at the time both sides denied that any money had been involved in Danny Gardella's decision to drop his case, it turned out later that in fact he had been paid a $60,000 settlement by the Major Leagues. He admitted, "I felt like I was getting paid off, but being a poor man I felt more or less justified. It wasn't like I had a lot of money and was being paid off." Gardella played only one game for the Cardinals during the 1950 season and was then sent down to the minor leagues and released after only a month. He returned to the Bronx, where, until his death in 2005, he worked as a sweeper in a warehouse, much as Judge Frank had predicted. In hindsight, one of the differences between Gardella's challenge and Curt Flood's two decades later was the former's lack of support from his fellow players. One of his fellow players in the Mexican Leagues, Mickey Owens, even expressed his hope that Gardella would lose his case. Others, like St. Louis Cardinals slugger Stan Musial, seemed satisfied with the system as it was. Whatever his motives may have been for bringing his suit and carrying it as far as he did, Gardella's challenge to the reserve system got organized baseball's attention. The possibility of a lengthy trial was certainly not appealing to team owners or the commissioner, and the circuit court's decision, especially Judge Frank's opinion, was especially troubling. Contrary to the reluctance expressed by Judge Chase, in his dissenting opinion in a lower court, to tell the Supreme Court "what to do," the Supreme Court during these years often followed the lead of lower federal courts, especially Chief Judge Learned Hand's Second Circuit. After all, that was exactly what the High Court had done in 1922 in the *Federal Baseball* case.

If organized baseball believed that the Gardella settlement had ended threats to the reserve system and its control over the careers of the players, it was mistaken. In the aftermath of his case, more judicial challenges would be brought and baseball would face a new threat in the form of a congressional investigation. Congressional involvement should not have been a complete surprise. Implicit in Judge Chase's lengthy dissent in the Gardella case was the possibility that the Supreme Court's "case by case" process for determining those businesses and activities covered under the provisions of the Sherman Act was not the only way to settle the issue. If the legislature had created an exemption by default, then Congress could eliminate that exemption by passing new legislation. In August 1951 Brooklyn Democratic congressman Emmanuel Celler, chairman of the House Judiciary Committee's Subcommittee on the Study of Monopoly Power, began holding a series of hearings to examine baseball and determine whether or not Congress needed to step in and remove its antitrust exemption. The ostensible reason for such hearings was three bills proposed in Congress that would have granted "blanket immunity from all antitrust laws," not only for baseball but for "all professional sports enterprises." However, it was clear that the bills themselves were in response to the Gardella case as well as a number of new pending lawsuits. According to one of the bill's sponsors, Senator Edwin Carl Johnson of Colorado, himself a minor league president, if these challenges to the reserve system by "disgruntled players" succeeded, "America's national pastime will be relegated to the sandlots from which it emerged a century ago." For Senator Johnson, the only thing that could prevent such a "tragedy" was legislative action. "I cannot think of a worse place to rest this matter than in the courts," he warned.

The case Senator Johnson referred to had been brought by George Toolson and several other minor league players. Toolson played for the New York Yankees minor league affiliate in Newark. When he was assigned to the lower Binghamton club at the start of the 1950 season, he refused to go, at which point he was placed on the "ineligible" list, in effect "blacklisted" from trying to find another team to play for. So he sued the Yankees, arguing that the reserve system illegally prevented him from furthering his career, especially since the Yankees team at this time was one of the most powerful in the Major Leagues and "loaded" with talented players. The federal district court dismissed the suit for lack of jurisdiction, and Toolson appealed the ruling to the Supreme Court. The case was pending as the Celler Committee began its work.

At various times between August and October 1951, the committee held its hearings to better understand the "intricacies of organized baseball." Beginning with one of the living legends of baseball, Ty Cobb, the committee heard from both league presidents, the commissioner, managers, players, and sports journalists. Although the hearings were widely publicized, the committee prohibited radio, television, and newsreel coverage of the proceedings. This was done in order to ensure that potential jurors in the pending Toolson case would not be influenced. Chairman Celler, a lifelong Brooklyn Dodgers fan, explained that he wanted to do what was "best for baseball" given the fact that the case represented "a sword of Damocles hanging over the head of our national pastime."

Invariably, witnesses before the committee were asked variations of the same question: Was baseball's reserve clause either "necessary," "essential," "fair," "reasonable," or "a must," and were witnesses "satisfied" with it? By and large, almost all answered in the affirmative, including the players themselves. Dodgers infielder Pee Wee Reese was typical. Not wanting to say anything against baseball because it had been "so wonderful to me," Reese agreed that without the clause, baseball couldn't operate. He also confirmed that most players agreed with that view and claimed he knew of no player who didn't. On May 27, 1952, the committee submitted its report on organized baseball to Congress. The report began with what was becoming almost a pro forma opening: "Baseball is America's national pastime." It went on to conclude that although there were some "undesirable consequences" of the reserve system, the "overwhelming preponderance of the evidence established baseball's need for some sort of reserve clause." At the same time, the committee rejected proposed legislation that would have given baseball a "blanket exemption" from antitrust laws, as such a law would preclude any resort to the courts in those rare instances where there might be abuse of the system. In the same vein, the report rejected the idea of creating a special governmental body or agency to regulate baseball. "Organized baseball," the committee concluded, was largely a "self-regulated industry," and a new government agency would be an "unwise" burden on both baseball and the American taxpayer. Finally, the Celler Committee expressed some interest in a possible middle ground between doing away with baseball's exempt status and making it complete. It suggested consideration of a limited exemption for the reserve clause consisting of "general legislation" that would enable clubs to promote competition while giving players a "reasonable opportunity" to advance their own careers and salaries. "This type of legislation would lay down a rule of reason for baseball." Having suggested a solution for the problem of the reserve rule, the Celler Committee then simply turned around and rejected its own reasoning! It would in fact be "premature" for Congress to pass such legislation until the "reasonableness of the reserve rules has been tested by the courts." Until the courts determined what was reasonable and unreasonable about the way organized baseball operated, "no legislative action" was recommended.

Congressman Celler had no need to worry about contaminating jurors in the *Toolson* case, as Toolson lost at the district and court of appeals levels. In October 1953 his case was argued before the Supreme Court, and less than a month later, in a single paragraph only slightly longer than the Court's 1922 ruling, the Court returned the favor to the Celler Committee. In a *per curium* opinion, the Supreme Court upheld *Federal Baseball,* this time noting that it was Congress that had considered baseball's antitrust exemption and had chosen not to make any change. In refusing to overrule *Federal Baseball,* the Supreme Court threw the ball back to Congress, arguing that if there were "evils in this field" that warranted the application of antitrust laws, "it should be by legislation."

Between congressional inaction and the Supreme Court's unwillingness to reconsider what most experts had by then conceded was a suspect decision, it must have seemed to the owners and managers who made up organized baseball in the 1950s that their campaign to transform baseball into *the* national pastime had succeeded, in spite of the fact that they had accomplished this goal by preserving a status quo that went back fifty years and more. But as G. Edward White has noted, organized baseball might have done well to look "beneath the surface." Baseball may have tried not to change, but America certainly had, and baseball might have to do so as well. One of the changes was demographic. Along with the post–World War II "baby boom," the late 1940s witnessed a seismic population shift within the country as Americans migrated from urban cores to the suburbs and from the Northeast and Midwest to the South and West. At the time Curt Flood began his career in professional baseball, St. Louis was the farthest western and southern Major League franchise. By the time of his lawsuit, there were teams in Los Angeles, San Francisco, Atlanta, Houston, and San Diego in the National League and in Oakland, California (Anaheim), Kansas City, and Seattle in the American League. Yet this expansion did not always contribute to the kind of image of baseball that the owners seemed so desperate to maintain. The move of the Dodgers and Giants was a blow to one of the country's most dedicated fan bases, and even the eventual return of baseball to Long Island with the Mets did little to assuage the hurt feelings of many thousands of New York and Brooklyn fans. The spectacle of the decamping of Washington's beloved Senators to Texas would take place the very year that Curt Flood's case was argued before the Supreme Court. Moreover, during the 1950s, as White and others have pointed out, actual attendance at baseball games declined. Thanks to television and continued radio broadcasts, fans could watch games in the comfort of their homes, without the hassles of traffic jams, aging public transport, and increasing prices of everything from tickets to hot dogs.

Another change that emerged in the 1950s, which would prove to be a more significant threat to organized baseball and its self-image as *the* American sport, was the growing popularity of other professional sports, especially football and basketball. The National Football League (NFL), which began in the 1920s, and the National Basketball Association (NBA), which dated from the 1940s, had by the 1950s begun to eclipse baseball in viewership, especially after embracing television. One advantage exploited by football and baseball was the fact that both sports, especially football, were already popular at the college level. Early on, both football and basketball bypassed organized baseball's development of a "farm system" by drafting the best college-level players. This eliminated the "developmental" expenses that Major League baseball teams incurred sponsoring affiliated minor league franchises.

Although the method of recruitment of new players differed, the NFL and NBA used hiring practices similar to those of organized baseball in the form of standard contracts that bound a player to a team for as long as that team wanted. Inevitably, then, the same question would have to be faced — the applicability of the antitrust statutes to these sports leagues. In 1957 a football player, George Radovich, sued the NFL, arguing just that. Radovich, a veteran player with the Detroit Lions football club, had requested a transfer to the Los Angeles team to be closer to his ailing father. The Lions refused the transfer, and when Radovich attempted to sign with a San Francisco team in the rival Pacific Coast League, the team was advised by the NFL that because Radovich had been "blacklisted" by the league when he had left the Lions, the San Francisco team would suffer "severe penalties" if it hired him. It did not hire him, and Radovich sued, arguing that football should not be exempt from antitrust laws.

On February 25, 1957, the Supreme Court in a 6-3 ruling held that football was subject to federal antitrust legislation. The majority in *Radovich v. National Football League, et al.*, concluded that *Federal Baseball* and *Toolson* applied only to baseball, and that since Congress had already chosen not to change baseball's exempt status, that status had to continue. Otherwise, Justice Tom Clark predicted without irony, there would be "a flood of litigation." The Court also cited its recent rulings that extended the antitrust laws to professional boxing and motion-picture theaters. For the Court, the "volume of interstate business" in each of these activities justified application of the antitrust acts. "Likewise, the volume of interstate business involved in organized professional football places it within the provisions of the Act." The Court conceded that this ruling could be considered "unrealistic, inconsistent, or illogical," were it not for those two baseball cases that the Court was bound under *stare decisis* to follow. In other words, were it not for *Federal Baseball*, baseball would most certainly have come under federal antitrust jurisdiction, just like boxing, movies, and now football. But *because* of that case and its reaffirmation in *Toolson*, only Congress could remove the sport's exempt status. In his dissenting opinion, Justice Felix Frankfurter, who in fact idolized Justice Holmes, pointed out that the majority's decision revolved far less around a particular enterprise and the Sherman Act than around what he called the "appropriate compulsion of *stare decisis*." He also noted that nowhere in the majority opinion was it ever explained how the "business" of baseball was in any way different from football and therefore not subject "equally" to the same laws.

A second dissent by Justices John M. Harlan and William Brennan stated outright what the majority had only implied. If the "situation" with respect to baseball's unique status was to be changed, it must be done by Congress. Either Congress should eliminate all distinctions between the various professional sports or by "discriminatory fiat" make baseball exempt. In fact, that was what happened. A number of bills were proposed to Congress, most of them variations of the same legislation considered five years earlier. During the summer of 1957 Congressman Celler's committee once again heard extensive testimony from persons involved in the game as well as players and officials from other sports. Many of the ballplayers testified that the reserve clause was necessary and that their fellow players were still "satisfied" with it. Stan Musial claimed that he "had studied this thing," and in his view no changes were necessary. He also testified that he had never heard "one complaint" from his fellow players. At least one player did speak out in favor of some change. Bob Feller, retired star pitcher for the Cleveland Indians, was at that time president of the Major League Baseball Players Association (MLBPA). Feller supported some modification of the reserve system that would allow a player "if he is dissatisfied with his team" to go "up for grabs" after a specific number of years with that team.

The committee hearings this time did result in sending a bill to the House for approval, but it was a compromise measure that rejected a complete removal of all sports from antitrust regulation and also rejected complete regulation. Under Celler's bill, all sports would be subject to federal antitrust laws except for those practices "reasonably necessary" for sports to maintain competition, preserve team hegemony geographically, manage television and broadcast rights, and "preserve the integrity of the game." Ultimately a substitute bill was approved by the House that eliminated the "reasonably necessary" phrase and specified the practices that would be exempt. The bill then went to the Senate, where during July 1958 another round of hearings was held, this time by Senator Estes Kefauver's Judiciary Committee's Subcommittee on Antitrust and Monopoly. These hearings, as the scholar Jerold J. Duquette concluded, "made up for lack of productivity with some very entertaining testimony," most notably that of New York Yankees star player Mickey Mantle and his manager Casey Stengel. When Senator Kefauver asked Mantle for his views on possible limits to the reserve system, Mantle replied, "I don't know. I don't think about this stuff very much [laughter]." He followed a lengthy, rambling testimony by the colorful Stengel, who kept the committee room laughing but provided little insight into the necessity or legality of the reserve clause. The Mantle-Stengel show was perhaps the high point of Congress's second attempt to deal with baseball and the reserve clause—which led to the same result as the first attempt. Nothing was done. The substitute bill (called the Walter-Keating Bill) was never acted upon by the Senate, and Congress would not become involved with baseball, antitrust, and the reserve clause for another thirty years.

Thus, by the end of the 1950s and the start of Curt Flood's career in professional baseball, the reserve system remained a fundamental part of the relationship between organized baseball and the players. The issue had become a "stalemate," or more appropriately had been tossed like a baseball back and forth between the courts and Congress in what promised to be a never-ending game of catch. During these years another set of changes took place that would have an impact on Curt Flood's case. These changes involved the structure and governance of organized baseball and the evolution of a strong, effective players' organization. The successors to baseball's first commissioner, Judge Kenesaw Landis, attempted to preserve the system of baseball governance much as Landis had left it, yet none had his leadership abilities or his dominant personality, especially over league presidents and team owners. After Landis's departure in 1944, there were three commissioners prior to 1968: Happy Chandler (1945–1951), Ford C. Frick (1951–1965), and William D. Eckert (1965–1968). Eckert had no baseball experience but had been a general in the U.S. Air Force (military procurement) and possessed a master's in business administration. Hired to make baseball a more efficient "business" operation, Eckert was confronted with the kind of challenges that he admitted he was unprepared to deal with, especially in the area of marketing and public relations. He also had to face a situation that no military commander would tolerate and corporate executives feared most: His "employees" organized. After just three years, Eckert was gone. His successor was Bowie K. Kuhn. A Washington, D.C., native (as a boy he had worked the scoreboard for the Washington Senators) and a University of Virginia Law School graduate, Kuhn became a partner in the law firm of Wilkie, Farr & Gallagher, which represented the National League. In 1966 he gained the attention of the nation, and the owners, when he successfully defended the league's transfer of the

Milwaukee Braves franchise to Atlanta in an antitrust lawsuit in the Wisconsin state courts.

Although he was a compromise candidate for the commissioner's post, upon his appointment in February 1969 Kuhn began immediately to implement the mandate he had been given by the owners to restructure the commissioner's office and the organization of baseball generally. Believing that for too long organized baseball had tended toward "complacency," Kuhn wanted to improve baseball's relationship with the press and broadcast media as well as with the fans. He recognized that the game itself needed more offensive action, as it had become "dominated" by pitching, and wanted to restructure the two leagues, each of which consisted at the time of ten teams. Finally, Kuhn was faced with something that his predecessors had not endured: "a players union militantly and skillfully led by Marvin Miller."

Kuhn was talking about the Major League Baseball Players Association. As described in earlier chapters, this was not the first time in the history of the sport that players had attempted to organize. Like its earlier counterpart, the MLBPA was created in 1953 to deal primarily with working conditions and player benefits, in this case the funding of players' pensions. It had only a part-time executive director, Frank Scott, and after 1960 a part-time legal consultant, Judge Robert Cannon. Representatives selected by each team met three or four times a year, and there was an association president, a position held by Bob Feller at the time of the 1957 congressional hearings. By and large, the MLBPA was viewed during these years as a "house union" that tended to follow the owners' agenda, and Judge Cannon especially came to be seen by players as being too close to the owners. According to the historian of the association, Charles P. Korr, Cannon thought of himself more as an "intermediary" between the owners and the players than as an "independent" voice on behalf of the players' concerns. By 1965 the MLBPA had concluded that it was time to hire a full-time director. After a contentious search, the association picked Marvin J. Miller to lead it. Born in the Bronx in 1917, Miller was a trained labor economist who had worked for the National War Labor Board during World War II, then had become a negotiator and analyst for the United Auto Workers. At the time of his selection in 1966, he worked with the powerful United Steelworkers union. Like baseball's commissioner, Miller faced the daunting challenge of bringing leadership and effective organization to a constituency that had its own form of complacency going back many years. For Miller and the players, it was an issue of "union solidarity." He admitted that "players were not only ignorant about unions, they were positively hostile to the idea: They didn't know what a union was, but they knew they didn't want one."

Neither man's appointment was universally applauded, especially by those with ties to either organized baseball or the players. One baseball manager, Paul Richards, famously remarked on Marvin Miller's appointment that "it is the end of baseball as we know it." It was a view shared by Commissioner Kuhn, who from their first dealings together found Miller to be "pedantic, fussing over details, and unwilling to deal straightforwardly with issues." For Kuhn, Miller was at heart an old-fashioned "trade unionist" who "hated" management, especially baseball's, and who often took on an "egalitarian pose" while always being willing to feed the press exaggerated if essentially true stories. Miller's feelings for Kuhn were similarly antagonistic. Miller saw Kuhn's appointment as commissioner as clear evidence of the owners' intent to "rid themselves" of the players' union or, if that were not possible, to disrupt or weaken it. Miller would later give Kuhn the ultimate insult disguised as praise by claiming that Kuhn "must be singled out as the single most important contributor to the successes of the Players Association." According to Miller, Kuhn was a poor leader, a bad tactician whose "moves always backfired," and someone who was unable to "distinguish between reality and his prejudices."

Despite this mutual distrust, or perhaps because of it, Kuhn and Miller, along with their legal advisers, Dick Moss of the MLBPA and John Gaherin of the commissioner's office, began discussions and negotiation that would lead to the first of a series of Basic Agreements. These agreements would not only redefine the relationship between baseball's owners and the players but would, as Richards had predicted, be the beginning "of the end of baseball as we knew it" — in some ways neither party might have predicted. At the very least, the rise of Marvin Miller and the MLBPA seriously undermined one of the basic operational tenets of professional baseball that had persisted since the days of Judge Landis and went back even further, to the A. G. Spaulding era. This tenet was the idea that the team owners had an unassailable monopoly on deciding what was "in the best interests" of baseball and what exactly was meant by the phrase "the good of the game," especially when it involved the players themselves.

The starting point for this process was the Basic Agreement of 1968, or the Collective Bargaining Agreement (CBA). Although, as Charles P. Korr pointed out, the agreement was "remarkably ordinary" as labor contracts went, it did establish the "credibility" of the MLBPA and Miller's leadership. The document included provisions on issues such as pension benefits and union dues that were already in place and at the same time opened up a range of issues and players' concerns to the bargaining process, including regular-season and playoff salaries and stipends, scheduling, and preseason expense stipends. Article 4 of the CBA provided that there would now be "a Grievance Procedure, the purpose of which is to set forth an orderly and expeditious system for the handling and resolving of grievances." The actual procedure for the "arbitration" of players' grievances was spelled out at great length, and like any contract, the CBA contained a number of clauses protecting the "rights" of both parties. Most importantly, it meant that the players could get a "fair hearing" for their grievances. Of course the one issue that Kuhn and the owners refused to include or make subject to any collective bargaining was the reserve clause. However, the agreement provided for the creation of a joint study committee on the reserve system, which began holding a series of meetings starting in April 1969. Over the next two years, nothing happened. At these meetings, Miller and the players' representatives on the committee proposed changes to the system, which the owners rejected out of hand. For the owners, the system was fundamental to baseball's existence, as history had shown and Congress and the courts had confirmed. Any possible modifications of the system were, in Charles B. Korr's apt characterization, "the baseball equivalent of Galileo questioning the earth-centered universe." The owners believed that anyone who criticized that system or proposed any changes or modifications could be doing so only for selfish financial gain.

The creation of the MLBPA, and Miller's leadership, became both a cause and an effect of Curt Flood's legal challenge. Without that organization's financial, moral, and legal backing, it is likely that Flood might never have been able to bring his lawsuit, let alone see it to its ultimate resolution. Curt Flood might well have chosen to retire quietly from baseball and pursue his other interests and talents, like Jackie

Robinson, or he might have been tempted back into baseball indirectly, much as Danny Gardella had been a decade earlier. It was to Marvin Miller's credit that in the meetings and discussions with Flood leading up to the lawsuit, he was honest and frank about Flood's chances and about the consequences for Flood personally. Miller would be there with Flood at each stage of the legal process. At the same time, it was fortuitous that Miller and the MLBPA were given the opportunity at that moment in time to bring further pressure on organized baseball — not only by challenging the reserve system but by getting the owners to take the ballplayers seriously. Bringing the owners and their minions into a courtroom where they would have to testify and be questioned under oath by no less than a former Supreme Court justice was not quite getting the home-field advantage, but for Flood and the players it may at least have made the playing field more level.

CHAPTER 5

The Trial

The trial in the case of *Curtis G. Flood v. Bowie Kuhn, et al.*, began on Tuesday, May 19, 1970, in Judge Irving Ben Cooper's fifteenth-floor courtroom in the Foley Square Federal Courts Building in lower Manhattan. As described in the press, the courtroom, with its high ceilings, polished wood, and green leather chairs, provided an "impressive setting" for the contest. Judge Cooper, who would not only be presiding but also deciding the case, was described as "a peppery, bald man with a fringe of white hair and a mustache." Born in London, England, in 1902, Judge Cooper had come to America at an early age, yet he often affected a "slightly British" accent. As noted in Chapter 1, he was known for being temperamental and for his courtroom outbursts. He had once called an attorney a "crummy little lawyer from the crummy little Legal Aid Society" and had referred to a group of youthful defendants as "punks." From the outset, the trial proceedings received extensive coverage in both local and national media outlets, which was not unexpected given the parties involved and the location of the trial. As had been true in the previous hearings, the language and imagery used both inside and outside the courtroom were punctuated with baseball and sports terminology. In describing Judge Cooper's dismissal of the owners' attorneys' opening motion to dismiss the case, the New York *Daily News* opined, "Lawyers for Curt Flood sent up two pinch-hitters in the sixth inning yesterday after Judge Irving Ben Cooper refused to call the game because of rain."

As befitted a contest involving baseball, both sides had "teams" of attorneys as impressive as the courtroom itself. As noted in Chapter 1, Flood's chief counsel was former Supreme Court Justice Arthur Goldberg, who was assisted by Jay Topkis from Goldberg's prestigious New York City firm Paul, Weiss, Goldberg, Rifkind, Wharton & Garrison. Also representing the plaintiff were Richard "Dick" Moss of the Major League Baseball Players Association and Allan Zerman, Flood's St. Louis attorney. At the defendants' table sat an even larger group of attorneys, including Mark F. Hughes and Louis L. Hoynes of the Wilkie, Farr & Gallagher firm, representing MLB and the National League, along with Victor Kramer of the Washington, D.C., powerhouse firm Arnold & Porter, representing Bowie Kuhn, and Sandy Hadden, representing the American League.

The plaintiff's first "lead-off" witness was Flood himself. Afterward he would characterize the trial as "dull," but on the stand the normally poised and articulate Flood appeared "tense" and "ill at ease." Justice Goldberg had barely begun his questioning when Judge Cooper broke in to admonish Flood to speak more loudly and slowly; this request would be repeated several times during his testimony. Flood's nervousness may not have only been the result of being in an unfamiliar environment. Ever since Judge Cooper back in February had denied Flood's motion for an injunction against baseball that would have allowed him to play in the 1970 season, Flood had been extremely upset. He wanted to play baseball, and not being able to play was a physical and emotional strain on both him and his friend Marian. His performance in court may also have been affected by a series of phone calls he had received just before the trial had begun. Monte Irvin, a former star player in both the Negro League and the Major Leagues who now worked for Commissioner Kuhn, had contacted Flood with a message from the commissioner. Kuhn wanted to meet with Flood in Los Angeles to explore the possibility of Flood playing for "any National League club of his choice without jeopardizing the litigation." Whether this offer had been an "open door" that would have allowed Flood to both play and keep his legal challenge alive or a trap, as Marian believed, designed to make his case "moot" before it ever reached trial was not clear. Flood turned the offer down, but it must have been on his mind as he began testifying.

Aside from Judge Cooper's interruptions, Flood's testimony was fairly straightforward and undramatic. He started by going through his career in baseball, although in recalling his record he had to be shown his bubble-gum card to refresh his memory of previous batting averages. He then recounted the circumstances of how he had been notified of his trade and that prior to the phone call and the letter from the general manager he had received no indication from the

72   { *Chapter 5* }

team that he was about to be traded. The key moment, of course, was when he was asked to explain why he had refused to be traded and instead brought his lawsuit. His response was the same one he had been giving to the media since January: "Well, I didn't think after twelve years I should be traded and treated like a piece of property." He concluded his testimony by admitting that although he had wanted to continue playing for the Cardinals, he was willing to play for another team as long as he had the choice of what team to play for and could pick the team that offered him the "best deal." He also explained that he hadn't wanted to leave St. Louis because of his photography and portrait business and said that not playing baseball that season had affected his playing skills.

The second witness to be called was Marvin Miller, the executive director of the MLBPA. Miller described the background and purpose of the association, referring to it as a "labor organization" made up of all players, managers, coaches, and trainers. He explained what he called the "reserve clause system," noting that there was no longer any specific "reserve clause" in the standard contract all players were required to sign. It was a "system" because the moment a young player signed this agreement, the Uniform Players Contract, he was subject to a set of rules that gave Major League Baseball "complete control" over him. These young players entered the system through a draft. Twice yearly, teams selected baseball players from high schools or colleges in this draft. Once informed that he had been drafted by a team, the young man had to deal exclusively with that club. Either a player signed a contract with that club on the terms it offered, or he refused. A player who refused would have to wait six months until the next draft, at which time he could be drafted by another club. Although in theory it was possible for a player to keep doing this until he was drafted by the team he wanted, in reality a player who turned down two such drafts would likely never play professional baseball.

Reading from a printed copy of the Major League Rules, Miller explained the various rules that constituted the "system." Judge Cooper followed along with his own copy of the rules, although at one point he protested "on behalf of the public" that the print was too small for him to easily read. Miller began with the Uniform Players Contract, which every player had to sign and which differed only in the amount of salary. A crucial section of the contract was 10(a), under which a club could offer a contract to a player on or after January 15 of each year. If there was no agreement between the player and the club by the following March 15 — that is, if the player did not agree to the salary offered — the club had the "option" to unilaterally renew the previous year's contract by simply notifying the player that it was doing so. The player then had ten days within which to sign the new/old contract, which included the same provision for the following year. The result, said Miller, was that as long as a club wanted to exercise this option, a player "has no say whatsoever in terms of what conditions he plays under." A player had only one alternative under such a system — to find another way to make a living.

Miller also testified about various other provisions of the Uniform Contract and the Major League Rules that made the system unilateral and inflexible. Players had to agree to play for that team only, with exceptions for certain postseason exhibition games and the all-star game. Players were prohibited during their entire contractual period from participating in any other professional sports activity, such as wrestling, football, basketball, or hockey. In order to preserve the competitive balance between teams, club rosters were limited to forty players, and any player on a team's roster, or "reserved list," could neither contact nor be contacted by any other team to discuss present or future employment. Illegal contact, or "tampering," as well as any violation of these rules carried penalties — two variations of "blacklisting." A player who failed to report to his team could be placed on a "restrictive list," and a player who was deemed to have violated the reserve system would be placed on a "disqualified list." The latter action meant they could "not play for any club in organized ball." When Miller explained that "organized ball" included all major and minor league clubs not only in the United States but in Japan as well, Justice Goldberg exclaimed that he hadn't realized that "internationalism had flourished that far."

Like almost all the witnesses who followed, Miller was asked to give his opinion of the system he had described. Not unexpectedly, he called it "unnecessarily and unduly restrictive." During cross-examination by defense counsel, Miller conceded that rules were necessary for any business to operate successfully and that he felt some modification of these rules could be made to "preserve the best interests of the club owners, the players, and the fans." Having made such a concession, he was then questioned about an even more contentious issue during the trial than the reserve clause itself: He was asked what "current" attempts had been made to come up with such modifications. Miller's response was categorical: "We have not to this day heard a single counter proposal or a proposal for any modification whatsoever in any of the various ramifications and rules that make up the reserve rule system." Baseball owners, Miller testified, liked things exactly as they were.

In redirect questioning by Jay Topkis, Miller was asked to describe in greater detail how players were initially drafted as well as the problems encountered by players who were traded and forced to move their families to a new place. Once more the owners' intransigence was highlighted:

> *Question (Topkis):* Have you sought in your negotiations [with owners] to make changes in the reserve system? *Answer:* Yes, for three years.
> *Question:* Have you made the slightest progress? *Answer:* None.
> *Question:* Have you made a variety of proposals? *Answer:* Yes.
> *Question:* Have the owners made one proposal? *Answer:* No.

After a day's recess, the second full day of the trial was taken up with the testimony of three ballplayers: Jackie Robinson, Hank Greenberg, and Jim Brosnan. As expected, all agreed that the reserve system was unfair and too restrictive. Robinson, who had attended the first day of the trial with his wife in a show of support for Flood, repeated much the same views he had expressed to the Celler Committee in 1953. The system was too "unilateral" and therefore gave players no options: They could either accept what they were offered or not play professional ball. Interestingly, neither at the Celler hearings nor during Flood's trial was Robinson asked about his experiences in the Negro League. During the questioning of the players, Judge Cooper broke in fairly regularly with his own questions, usually asking the witnesses to further explain what they had just said. He referred to the players as the "experts" and seemed especially interested in getting them to be more specific regarding the reasons why they believed the reserve system was unfair and bad for the players and the game. Of the three players, Hank Greenberg probably came closest to clearly explaining his reasons. Greenberg had a unique status — not only had he been an outstanding Hall of Fame player with the Detroit Tigers but after his playing career he had been part of the management and ownership of two ball clubs: the Cleveland Indians and the Chicago White Sox. Greenberg believed that the reserve system was unfair particularly to average players and the young, "inexperienced" players who without any counsel or assistance, were forced to sign a contract at the very beginning of their careers that would bind them to a team for life.

Greenberg also explained that the reserve system was equally unfair to players at the other end of their careers. In fact, Greenberg had had an experience similar to Curt Flood's. After playing with the Tigers for sixteen years, Greenberg had been notified "by telegram" that he had been traded to the Pittsburgh Pirates. He had of course gone, but it had been difficult, not only for him as a player — especially because he was going to a different league — but also for all the Detroit fans among whom he was highly popular and respected. Looking back on this experience, Greenberg said he felt that a player who played for one team for a long period — especially when his performance was outstanding — developed a relationship with that club that should entitle him to have some say in his future. He called this a form of "building equity" and said that the relationship between players and their teams built on this equity was undermined when a player was suddenly traded and had absolutely no say in where or under what circumstances he would be playing. Greenberg felt that the owners were less concerned about players' interests than they should or could be. He concluded that elimination of the reserve clause would be an important step in enhancing baseball's "image."

Under cross-examination by Mark Hughes, Greenberg was pressed as to what would replace the reserve system if it were to be eliminated. In particular, he was questioned about the costs and length of time a team "invested" in developing a young player. Why, he was asked, would a club spend thousands of dollars for a young man to play several years in its minor league affiliate only to have that player end up playing for some other Major League team? Greenberg conceded that it often took more time to develop a newly drafted young baseball player than to develop, say, young football or basketball players, although he didn't believe it took as long as Hughes claimed. Moreover, in both of those other sports, players drafted were generally already star performers at the college level. This distinction was emphasized when Greenberg was questioned by Justice Goldberg on redirect and was able to make the telling point, based on his management experience, that baseball owners were able to "write off" developing players' salaries as expenses!

The entire third day of the trial was taken up with the testimony of Robert R. Nathan, a well-regarded professional economic consultant from Washington, D.C., hired by Flood's attorneys to analyze the broader economic impact of baseball's reserve system and its relationship to antitrust policies. Overall, Nathan contended that the reserve clause system tended to stifle competition, much as other forms of trusts and monopolies did for other aspects of America's free-market economy. He stated that eliminating the reserve system and replacing it with a multiyear contract — say, five years, at which time a player would presumably be free to negotiate with other teams — would in fact be "advantageous in the distribution of player talent among teams." But he was careful to deny that the effect of such a change would "equalize competition" among the teams. Rather, it would equalize the opportunities for teams to "be responsive in what happens in their competition and negotiations for players." Contrary to one of the owners' biggest fears, ending the reserve system would not result in the concentration of the best players on a few of the richest teams. When Judge Cooper interrupted to express his surprise at such an idea, Nathan responded that there was an "old saying in economics that we move from shirtsleeve to shirt sleeve in three generations." Certain firms or businesses do well for a time but then, because of other factors such as leadership and innovation, are gradually replaced. He cited the Milwaukee Braves as an example of a team that played in a much smaller city than Philadelphia or New York yet managed to have successful records and high attendance numbers. Nathan maintained that in the long run, a fixed-term contractual period of three to five years, after which a player could negotiate with other teams, would enhance competition in player performance both individually and as an "assembly" of players and talents — teams.

Under intensive cross-examination by Louis Hoynes, Nathan admitted that he had been hired just two weeks prior to the trial by Justice Goldberg and that his preparation had been based largely on material he had used earlier in a baseball case involving the Milwaukee franchise, including the report of the Celler Committee back in the 1950s. He also conceded that although he was "familiar" with the MLBPA, he was not very knowledgeable about the process by which players negotiated their contracts. In fact, he thought that aside from pensions and benefits, the association played no role in salary negotiations. However, Nathan insisted that the minimum salaries and maximum cuts that had been negotiated by the association with the owners were not enough. The situation in which players had "no alternative" in their employment choice did "substantially" reduce their "bargaining strength" relative to that of the teams. Finally, he was asked to defend the idea of multiyear contracts against the likely "tension" that it would create between a player's individual talent and performance (and greed?) versus the overall good of the team. Here of course was the fundamental danger that baseball owners and their supporters in the media and the public had been summoning up since the beginning of organized baseball. If not for the reserve system, players would care only for their "individual records" and improving them to get higher salaries from other teams. They would care only about themselves and not the good of their team. From "an economic point of view," it was difficult to rebut this notion because baseball had never tried an alternative. Nathan could only point out that if a player were "self-interested . . . egotistic . . . and disregards the interests of the team," his "reputation" would become known to other teams, and that would affect his ability to move to other teams as freely as feared. Finishing up, the economist was asked whether or not having a fixed-term contract system would place more emphasis on "individual achievement." "It might, Mr. Hoynes," Nathan replied.

The next set of witnesses called on Flood's behalf included the heads of three major sports leagues: Alva "Pete" Rozell of the National Football League, Walter Kennedy of the National Basketball Association, and Clarence Sutherland Campbell of the National Hockey League.

The questions put to these witnesses focused on their various systems of player drafting and what players could do after being with a team for a certain number of years. Essentially, these leagues operated under what they termed a "free agency" or "option reserve" system. With variations, this meant that after a player had been with a team for a certain number of years, he was free to explore playing for another team. All these executives agreed that baseball's reserve clause system was clearly out of date and that, based on their experiences, owners' fears of chaos and bankruptcy if the reserve system were eliminated or modified were groundless.

Other than Hank Greenberg, the only baseball owner called by Flood's attorneys as a witness was Bill Veeck Jr. The son of a former president of the Chicago Cubs, Veeck had grown up in the world of baseball management and over the course of his career had owned several Major League franchises (one, the White Sox, twice). He was considered one of the most iconoclastic and flamboyant baseball owners of his time. His "innovations" to the game, intended to attract larger crowds, were legendary. He had once hired a midget to come to bat in order to get a base on balls, and he had installed a new scoreboard in Chicago's Comiskey Park that exploded with fireworks every time a Sox player hit a home run. He had no great affection for the St. Louis Cardinals or owner Auggie Busch. He believed that back in the 1950s, when he had been the owner of the St. Louis Browns, the Cardinals had engineered the demise of the Browns' franchise. Although Veeck was the only witness other than Flood who referred to the reserve system and baseball as "one of the few places in which there is human bondage," he conceded that the complete elimination of that system would not be "helpful." Veeck would have adopted either football's system or what he called the "Hollywood contract," in which an actor signed with a studio for a period of years or number of pictures. In his cross-examination of Veeck, defense attorney Kramer focused less on the reserve system in general and more on getting Veeck to talk about Flood's career, especially the likelihood that without the system, Flood would not have been traded from Cincinnati to St. Louis and therefore would not have been "able to show his stuff" to the Cardinals.

On the sixth day, the defense began its case with Commissioner Bowie Kuhn. Over the next two days, Kuhn attempted to set out baseball's case for the reserve system. His defense essentially consisted of two parts—a historical justification and a practical one. Historically, Kuhn maintained, the reserve system had been instrumental in creating the sport of professional baseball "as we know it." During those periods when it was not used, there had been "chaos" as players moved from team to team, fans lost interest and trust in the game's "integrity," and teams went bankrupt. Kuhn also attacked as "objectionable" any modifications to the system, as they were either "unworkable" or would undermine the integrity of the game by interfering with the goal of "even competition." With his lawyer's background, he firmly believed that the Supreme Court's long-standing exemption of baseball from antitrust laws should continue. Kuhn's second line of defense was to show that lawsuits such as Flood's were unnecessary inasmuch as ballplayers had already achieved better conditions in the form of pensions, minimum salaries, and other protections and benefits. At the same time, Kuhn's testimony, contrary to much of the pretrial publicity and maneuvering, avoided criticizing Flood for bringing his lawsuit. "He [Flood] is perfectly free," Kuhn testified, "to sue anybody he wants. I don't criticize him for doing it or not as he sees fit." The primary object of Kuhn's ire was the MLBPA, which in his view had made a "serious mistake" in supporting Flood's suit. Over the past several years, the commissioner contended, baseball players had received considerable benefits through the process of "collective bargaining." In fact, the owners' bargaining team had been talking with the association about modifications at the time that the MLBPA had decided to support Flood. For Kuhn, this was evidence that the association was not seriously committed to "realistic negotiation" with the owners. The accusation that the association had been acting in "bad faith" would be repeated by Joe Cronin, president of the American League; by National League president Chub Feeney; and most heatedly by John Gaherin, the owners' representative in labor negotiations.

Despite the seriousness of the issues at stake in the trial, it was clear that Judge Cooper did not mind a bit of levity in the courtroom; as a result, the trial was punctuated with moments of humor, with the judge sometimes the instigator. Former player Jim Brosnan, one of Flood's witnesses, had been describing how as a result of the reserve system, he was sent back and forth between the major and minor leagues by his Chicago Cubs team. One time, when he was called back after only a week with the Cubs' minor league affiliate in Des Moines, his wife threatened to divorce him because she had just purchased two weeks' worth of steaks, and she wanted to know what she was supposed to do with them. When asked "for the record" what had happened to the steaks, Brosnan deadpanned, "She gave them to the player who reported to Des Moines in my place." Another witness whose jokes were described as having enlivened the proceedings was Joe Garagiola. Garagiola, a former baseball player who had become a popular television personality, was the only player called by the defense. He testified that the reserve system was "the best system so far and I haven't heard anyone come up with a better one." At one point Judge Cooper interrupted Garagiola's testimony to inquire why the former player was always smiling and wondered aloud what his reaction to the judge might be. Garagiola replied, "I like you, Judge, I wish you were on a bubble-gum card — I'd save you." Garagiola's testimony lasted only thirteen minutes (Flood's attorneys had no questions for him), and as he stepped down he was heard to utter in "mock chagrin" that "I can't even get to play a full game." Such lighter moments included the attorneys as well. During Bowie Kuhn's cross-examination by Jay Topkis, Kuhn denied being a "trained economist" despite his degree in economics from Princeton. Kuhn said, "There's a difference between a degree in economics from Princeton and being a trained economist." Kuhn's attorney jumped to his feet and exclaimed, "Your honor, as a Harvard man, I agree with that."

The last several days of the defense's case were taken up with testimony by a number of team owners, including Robert Reynolds of the Los Angeles Angels, Frank Dale of the Cincinnati Reds, John McHale of the Montreal Expos, and Ewing Kauffman of the Kansas City Royals. For the most part, all agreed that the reserve system as it existed was necessary for the "economic health" of their businesses. The owners of the newer franchises, Reynolds and McHale, were particularly adamant that they would not have considered investing in their enterprises had it not been for the system. After "long stretches of corroborative and technical testimony," the trial ended on June 10, at which time Judge Cooper began considering the more than two thousand pages of transcript and almost sixty evidentiary exhibits submitted. It was likely that it would be at least several weeks before he rendered his decision, so there was some speculation that some sort of settlement might be reached in the interim.

Two months later, on August 12, 1970, Judge Cooper issued his ruling in the case. In a forty-seven-page opinion, he ruled in favor of the defendants on all four of the claims he had agreed to consider (he had earlier rejected a fifth "unrelated" cause of action against the Cardinals and the New York Yankees). In determining whether or not the reserve system was "unduly restrictive," as the plaintiffs claimed, or "reasonable and necessary," as the defense argued, Judge Cooper concluded that the "preponderance of credible evidence" presented at the trial supported the latter. He noted that the plaintiff had failed to show that the system "occasioned rampant abuse" and specifically cited Robinson's and Greenberg's testimony as evidence that, aside from Flood himself, no one who had testified had called for the complete elimination of that system.

As to whether or not baseball was exempt from the antitrust statutes, Judge Cooper repeated the conclusion from his earlier ruling that only Congress or the Supreme Court could remove that exemption. However, in support of this ruling the judge now cited a case that had been decided by the Second Circuit Court of Appeals the previous month. The case, *Salerno and Valentine v. American League of Professional Baseball Clubs, et al.*, involved a suit against the American League by two umpires, Al Salerno and Bill Valentine. As a result of their attempts to organize American League umpires, as had already been done for National League umpires, the two veteran umpires had been fired by Cronin. Although the case had been going on for more than a year, it had received far less publicity and interest than Flood's case, most likely because it involved only one league and umpires were not one of the more popular groups working in baseball. Although they eventually won their right to organize, the circuit court had ruled once again that baseball was exempt from the antitrust statutes, and it was this part of the opinion that Judge Cooper referred to in denying Flood's antitrust claims. In his opinion in *Salerno and Valentine*, Judge Henry Friendly admitted that the 1922 *Federal Baseball* decision had not been "one of Mr. Justice Holmes' happiest days" and added that "we would not fall out of our chairs with surprise" if the Supreme Court overruled *Federal Baseball* and the *Toolson* decisions. However, just as in previous cases since 1922, he concluded that "we continue to believe that the Supreme Court should retain the exclusive privilege of overruling its own decisions." For Judge Cooper, this decision provided a clear "mandate" for denying the plaintiff's federal antitrust claim.

Judge Cooper's opinion rejecting Flood's other three claims was based entirely on the case law and legal doctrines found in the two sides' written briefs. He accepted the owners' argument that if the reserve clause was a "mandatory subject" of collective bargaining, it was therefore exempt from federal labor antitrust laws. Similarly, he held that if federal antitrust law did not apply to organized baseball, then baseball fell within the area "preempted from state regulation" as well. In support of this conclusion, Judge Cooper cited a Wisconsin state court ruling, *State v. Milwaukee Braves*, which held that "organized baseball operates widely in interstate commerce." As such, Judge Cooper reasoned, the reserve system was not a subject that admitted of "diversity of treatment." State and local regulations that "unduly burden" interstate commerce or "impede the free flow of commerce from state to state" were unconstitutional, even if, as in this case, Congress had not acted. In other words, as long as Congress and the Supreme Court had seen fit to exempt baseball from antitrust laws, no individual state or states could remove that exemption.

The fourth and final cause of action rejected by Judge Cooper was Flood's contention that the reserve system was a form of "involuntary servitude" prohibited by the Thirteenth Amendment. Since testimony presented during the trial had involved neither the Thirteenth Amendment nor even race, the judge relied again on case law and judicial interpretations of what constituted "involuntary servitude." For Judge Cooper, the key element "prerequisite to proof" of involuntary servitude was a showing of "compulsion." Flood, in Judge Cooper's view, had not been compelled to play for Philadelphia. He had had a choice, although admittedly the choice had been between playing for a team he did not want to play for or embarking on a "different enterprise outside organized baseball." Being forced to leave baseball, Judge Cooper wrote, may have meant a financial loss for Flood, but it was not proof of compulsion.

Having rejected all of Flood's claims, Judge Cooper then "unburdened" himself of some additional "convictions" he had formed during the course of the trial. In legal terms, this ten-page section of his opinion was "dicta"; that is, material not germane to the specific legal claims being ruled upon. Titling the section "The Conflicts Are Reconcilable," Judge Cooper started out by expressing his opinion that both sides presented witnesses who were "credible and of high order," and that both sides exhibited a "genuine enthusiasm" for baseball and had the "best interests of the game at heart." Given this circumstance, it was Judge Cooper's sincere conviction that negotiation between the parties could produce "an accommodation" on the reserve system that would be "eminently fair and equitable to all" and that would result in what he termed "continuity with change." Citing trial testimony, including that of players such as Greenberg and Robinson, he said he believed that both sides envisioned something between the complete elimination of the system and the status quo. Judge Cooper therefore urged both sides to negotiate changes on their own. He noted that oftentimes more complicated matters with far more hostile parties found their way to out-of-court settlements. "Why not here," he asked, "with the parties positive and reasonable men who are equally watchful over a common objective, the best interest of baseball?" In hindsight, Judge Cooper's dictum was prescient in regard to the ultimate fate of baseball's reserve system. At the time, it was seen by Miller and others as further evidence that Judge Cooper had harbored a discernible bias in favor of the owners.

Judge Cooper's ruling was not completely unexpected; both sides had understood from the beginning that the reserve clause issue and baseball's exemption from federal antitrust laws would ultimately have to be decided by the Supreme Court. The judge also seemed to recognize this, beginning his opinion by claiming that he had "resolved to allow great liberality in the making of the total trial record to the end that each theory or contention advanced by the litigants would be amply covered and dealt with when all the proof is in." Trials are also a form of contest with winners and losers, and usually the losing side does not like to lose. In his 1991 memoir *A Whole Different Ball Game*, Marvin Miller attempted to explain Flood's defeat, if only to prevent the "same mistakes" from being made again. He did allow that there was "no reason to complain" about the outcome of the trial because even he agreed with Judge Cooper's assertion that it was rare for a district court to overturn a Supreme Court ruling. Moreover, he noted that from the beginning Justice Goldberg had advised Flood and Miller that the "only way we could win was to fight it out all the way to the Supreme Court."

According to Miller, one important reason the trial's outcome was not surprising was the fact that Judge Cooper was the "prime example" of judges in this case allowing their "awe of baseball" to influence their legal decisions, or at least "their awe of being in a situation where their verdict could have a lasting impression on the national pastime." Miller noted Judge Cooper's use of baseball terminology but was especially upset at his "baiting" of Flood during his testimony, as when Judge Cooper had told Flood that testifying "isn't as easy as playing center field, is it?" In the context of the trial, such criticism was warranted. Judge Cooper made rich use of such terminology throughout the trial and began his opinion by stating, "Baseball is our national pastime and has been for well over a century." In that, and in his inability or unwillingness to entertain the possibility that baseball was as much a business as a "pastime," he certainly reflected the prevailing notion of the game's unique and exalted status in American society. However, Judge Cooper's use of baseball terminology was no different from the approach taken by the media, and one has only to look at the records and reports of the Celler Committee hearings on baseball in the 1950s to see that judges were not the only government officials whose particular enthusiasm and reverence, whether real or momentary, for baseball and those involved in it ran deep (not to mention the tradition of presidents throwing out the first baseball of the season). If what Judge Cooper felt was awe, then it was the kind of awe experienced by much of American society in 1970. And if, as Paul Finkelman has argued, "the culture of baseball is emphatically the culture of the rule of law," then Judge Cooper's behavior and language were not that surprising. When, for example, he referred to court recesses as "seventh-inning stretches," he was certainly demonstrating this intersection of legal and baseball cultures. (Purists might argue that a "time out" is the more appropriate equivalent to a court recess because it's up to the discretion of the umpire, whereas the seventh-inning stretch always occurs between halves of the seventh inning.) As will be seen, it would not be the last time a judge would behave in such a manner.

Miller admitted that "we made mistakes in the case" as well, and one of the biggest was not having the players take "a more visible and active part in the trial." The executive director of the MLBPA felt that the "media appeal" of having more ballplayers, especially the more famous ones, testify would have put a more human face on his organization and its case for the public. It was indeed curious that only three players testified on Flood's behalf and that two of them, Robinson and

Greenberg, were veterans. Miller explained the failure to have more currently active players take the stand by pointing out that the trial had taken place during the regular season and he hadn't wanted to distract players from their work. It may be worth noting that while the trial was going on, the New York Yankees were in town and played series against the Chicago White Sox and the Kansas City Royals. But Miller also admitted that the virtual absence of those most directly affected by the reserve system was his own "failure of leadership." Miller had been derelict in convincing the players who made up the association that each and every one of them had an important stake in what Flood was doing, and that they needed to support that effort actively and publicly. At the same time, he recognized that most players either "didn't care" about the outcome of the case or, especially in the case of marginal players, were fearful of retaliation by their teams if they were more "visible" supporters.

Certainly from the outset of the case, Judge Cooper displayed an enthusiasm and personal involvement that seemed at times to cross the boundaries of judicial impartiality and neutrality. In his opinion, he wrote about baseball as "our" national pastime. But to say he was in "awe" of baseball, as Miller described him, suggests that the judge was intimidated by the defendants' side from the beginning and therefore believed that "the ball was too hot to handle, so he was going to toss it onto the next court." Aside from Miller himself resorting to another sports metaphor, the implication was that Judge Cooper's "awe" meant he had no intention of deciding the "hot" issues before him, especially the reserve clause. But "our national pastime" also included the players, and Judge Cooper's interjections and questions to the players called by Flood's attorneys reflected a kind of awe as well — at least in the sense that Judge Cooper referred to the players as "the experts" and was almost eager for them to explain exactly why the reserve system was unreasonable. In his opinion, Judge Cooper noted that instances of abuse of the system were not "rampant," but since he had heard testimony about only one instance — Flood's — he could hardly conclude otherwise. The judge also noted that with the exception of Flood, many of the plaintiffs' own witnesses had conceded that some sort of reserve system was "necessary." Had a lineup of players testified that the reserve clause was too restrictive, and had there been testimony from them about how the clause actually affected their lives and careers, at least there would have been a stronger record for Flood's position. As it was, Judge Cooper was left with the MLBPA position, not that of the individual players who made up the organization. And since the purpose of the association and the Basic Agreement had been to create a process for collective bargaining to negotiate between organized baseball and the players, the judge's "dicta" that the two sides could and should negotiate "an accommodation on the reserve system which would be eminently fair and equitable to all concerned" was probably naive but not necessarily unwarranted.

In fact, Judge Cooper ended his opinion, and his own involvement in *Flood v. Kuhn*, by resorting to one last baseball allusion, one that demonstrated the intersecting cultures in the most important way: the notion of a judge as a kind of umpire. "We are bound by the law as we find it," he stated, "and by our obligation to call it as we see it." With the district court having handed down its opinion "constituting its findings of fact and conclusions of law in favor of the defendants," it was now up to Flood's attorneys to take the next step. On August 24, 1970, they filed a notice of appeal to the Second Circuit Court of Appeals in Manhattan. As Leonard Koppett put it, "Flood Whiffs, Goes into Extra Innings."

CHAPTER 6

"The Senator from Copenhagen"

Despite initial expectations on both sides of a lengthy court battle possibly stretching over years, Curt Flood's case had thus far proceeded, in Marvin Miller's words, more like "Willie Mays going from first to third." After filing their appeal with the circuit court in August, Flood's attorneys were notified that oral arguments were to be scheduled for the end of January. That was less than half the normal time between a filing and the hearing in the federal courts in civil actions like theirs. But between the end of trial and the circuit court hearings, a number of things happened that, although they didn't necessarily directly affect the outcome of Flood's case, had long-term consequences for both him and baseball.

On May 21, 1970, two days after Flood's trial began, the owners and the Major League Baseball Players Association reached accord on a new Basic Agreement. On June 4, just two days before the trial ended, it was announced that the MLBPA membership had agreed by an overwhelming vote of 541 to 54 to approve the new document. This agreement made a number of substantive changes to the original Basic Agreement, approved back in 1968, as described in Chapter 4. The new agreement included increases in players' minimum salaries, adjusted increases in income from postseason playoff games, larger stipends for meals and spring training expenses, and moving-expense stipends for players traded during the season based on the geographic distance between their old and new clubs. The agreement also increased the limits (20 percent from the previous year and 30 percent from two prior years) that teams could *reduce* a player's salary in any given year. It also reset payments for players, based on their annual salaries at the time, who were terminated during spring training (thirty days) or during the season (sixty days).

The new Basic Agreement also included a provision that dealt specifically with the reserve system, but in a most peculiar way. Article 14 of the compact stated that "this Agreement does not deal with the reserve system." It recognized that the "parties [to the Agreement] have differing views as to the legality and the merits of such system as presently constituted"; therefore, until the "final and unappealable adjudication (or voluntary discontinuance)" of Flood's case, neither party would take "concerted action" with respect to that issue. Further, the provisions also recognized that this new agreement should "in no way prejudice the position or legal rights" of either side with respect to the reserve system. In other words, as long as the case went on, the reserve system was still in place. However, since neither the players nor the owners could predict the outcome of the case, a section of the article also included provisions for the reopening of negotiations on the system should there be a final adjudication (or discontinuance) of the case. At the same time, the article recognized that prior to the expiration of the agreement, a final resolution of the case might occur, and it might be decided against the reserve system. Therefore, depending on whether such a ruling or outcome occurred before or after October 1 (the starting date for player contract negotiations under the system), provisions were made for the "re-opening" of negotiations between the association and the owners. Whether or not this article was evidence of the owners' continuing unwillingness to make any good-faith effort to deal with the reserve system, it at least suggested that Flood's case, and his and the association's demonstrable willingness to fight "to the finish," had by now gotten their attention.

The possibility that Flood and the association might discontinue their legal challenge to the reserve system was further clouded by another development after the trial: Curt Flood returned to professional baseball. As noted in Chapter 5, he had found the trial "dull" and, aside from Jackie Robinson's appearance on his behalf, had considered it less significant than the written briefs and the constitutional and legal arguments submitted that would ultimately be examined by the Supreme Court. He was, however, still determined to continue. "I have promised to pursue the matter to the Supreme Court of the United States, if necessary. I have no choice. The owners left me none." But it was clear that the case was taking its toll on him. He spent the summer of 1970 before Judge Cooper's ruling came out, in his words, "bedding and boozing." He avoided any "gainful pursuits" because he feared that such activity would be interpreted as a sign that he knew he was going to lose. If that was not enough, he was reminded by the person closest to him, Marian Jorgensen, that his business dealings in St. Louis were in serious financial trouble. In fact, in June Flood's St. Louis corporation, Curt Flood Associates, Inc., and his Chicago partner company, Midwest School Pictures, Inc., had become defendants themselves in a suit filed by several businessmen in federal district court in St. Louis. The plaintiffs were asking for $150,000 in damages. Ashamed to go back to St. Louis, where he admitted he had once acted like a "hot-shot," Flood decided instead to "clear out" and head to Copenhagen. For Marian, who had shared his apartment in New York and had been his primary caretaker and support since his decision not to be traded, this would be her "liberation" as well as his. She could now go home to Oakland and resume her life. "I had," he confessed, "been exploiting her terribly."

In Copenhagen, a city that he had fallen in love with in 1968 on his way home from a Cardinals exhibition trip to Japan, Flood "played the artist," complete with beret and newly grown goatee. He also considered buying a club or restaurant. But then he received word of Judge Cooper's decision, and suddenly Copenhagen looked to him more like a "jail" than a vacation spot. He was now "on the lam," and between the lawsuits against him and his lawsuit against baseball having suffered its first defeat, he wondered, "Was the black champion of players' rights suppose to end like this—hiding from creditors in a Danish hotel room"? It was then that Flood got another phone call— two, actually. The first came from a *Washington Post* reporter to ask what Flood thought about the "deal." "Deal?" he answered. The reporter explained that the Washington Senators had been given the rights to negotiate with Flood in exchange for giving Philadelphia a player. Right after that, Robert "Bob" Short, the owner of the Senators, called to invite Flood back to New York to talk about returning to baseball. Curious and anxious to return to the States to play baseball again and do "his thing," Flood flew back to New York. Upon his return, he was asked by a reporter if Short's phone call had convinced him that " 'America is a nice place to live after all.' " Flood replied, "I didn't need Bob Short to convince me of that."

The "deal" the reporter spoke about had probably begun to take shape the previous spring. When Flood had first refused Philadelphia's offer in October 1969, under the league rules the Phillies still had exclusive rights to his services and he could not negotiate with any other team. Since he had not signed with the Phillies by January 15, 1970, his previous contract with the Cardinals — which in essence was what had been traded — was automatically renewed, and Flood was one of the forty players each team was allowed to carry on its reserve list, now as a "restricted" player. This meant he was not playing for Philadelphia but could not be contacted by any other team. However, that spring the Phillies renegotiated the trade with St. Louis and agreed to take two minor league players in place of Flood. At that point Flood was placed on their voluntary retirement list, which did not count toward the forty-players-per-team limit but still prevented Flood from playing for anyone else. According to Phillies general manager John Quinn, Bob Short first broached the idea of trading for Flood that spring. But without permission from Kuhn, and given the fact that Flood's case had yet even to go to trial, nothing more was done at the time. (Curiously, it may be recalled that just before the trial began, Flood was contacted by Monte Irvin to meet with Kuhn to discuss the possibility of Flood playing for a "National League team" of his choice. The Senators were in the American League.)

Bob Short was a Midwestern businessman who had recently purchased the moribund and hapless Senators (actually, it was the second incarnation of the team that had come from Minneapolis in 1960). Short's strategy to resuscitate the franchise (if that was in fact his goal, considering the fact that three years after he bought the team, he moved it to Texas) seemed to emphasize stocking his roster with well-known veteran players, the most prominent example being his hiring of the legendary, and retired, Boston Red Sox slugger Ted Williams as the team's manager. At the 1969 World Series in Cincinnati, the possibility of a trade for Flood again came up in conversations between Quinn and Short. Short indicated that he would be "happy" to discuss a deal, but first he needed to get approval from the commissioner. This seemed likely to happen because just the week before, Short had managed to "induce" Kuhn to reinstate another aging veteran player, the pitcher Denny McLain, so that Short could obtain him from the Detroit Tigers.

Once back in New York, Flood consulted with Marvin Miller. His obvious concern was whether or not his case would be affected if he went ahead and successfully negotiated a deal with the Senators. Miller, as "supremely objective" as always, told Flood that the decision, like his initial one to file the lawsuit, was up to him. However, Miller did advise Flood to speak with Goldberg before doing anything more. Goldberg, who at the time was in the middle of his unsuccessful campaign for governor of New York, met with Flood and gave him the go-ahead to sign. Goldberg explained that since Flood had sat out the entire 1970 season, he had already suffered sufficient damages (his $100,000 salary) that the appeals court would not find his claims against the reserve system moot. "I therefore think," the former justice told him, "that you can play in 1971 without hurting your case in the higher courts."

Before Flood's meeting with Short, another hitch appeared. It seemed that Philadelphia fans were unhappy with Quinn's trade and the prospect of losing a star like Flood in exchange for a single unknown player. It transpired that by approving the trade, Kuhn had violated two of the Major Leagues' own rules. The first was that a team could not trade a player in exchange for giving the other team the right to negotiate with that player. It had to be a player-for-player transaction. The second rule involved Short's promise to give Philadelphia an additional player in the form of the Senators' pick in the upcoming December draft. This promise of a future draft pick was a "football gimmick" that was prohibited by baseball's rules. When this came out, the Phillies were "embarrassed" and tried to get out of the deal. However, Kuhn was by now publicly committed to making sure Flood returned to baseball, especially since he had already approved Short's going ahead with the deal. Kuhn also believed that getting Flood to sign a contract with the reserve clause in it would not affect the case but might take some of the public "onus" off the owners' side. On October 30, Kuhn met with Short and Quinn, and a revised trade was arranged in which, in exchange for Flood, Philadelphia received three Washington minor league players.

With the trade now approved and with Goldberg's assurance that he would not be jeopardizing his legal case, Flood, along with Miller; Goldberg; Dick Moss; and Max Gitter, an attorney in Goldberg's firm, met with Bob Short at the beginning of November. Commissioner Kuhn was "involved" in the negotiations through Sandy Hadden, who had been the American League's attorney during the trial but now served on the commissioner's staff. At Goldberg's suggestion, Short agreed to pay Flood a salary of $110,000, a $10,000 increase over what he would have made with Philadelphia. Short also agreed, verbally, to give Flood a job during that winter with his St. Petersburg club in the Florida International League to help him with his financial situation and with getting in shape for the upcoming spring training season. The biggest sticking point, it seems, was the contract itself. Flood had wanted a provision in his contract that he could not be traded by the Senators without his consent. Kuhn insisted that any contract other than the standard Uniform Players Contract would not be approved, and as had been explained at the trial, the only blank space on the Uniform Contract was the salary line. But the commissioner also conceded that special provisions were sometimes added at the bottom of the form. The contract Flood ultimately signed on November 3, 1970, included the clause, but it was agreed that a separate covenant would be worked out that would include a provision that the owners would not use his signing against him as the lawsuit progressed through the courts. He also was assured that he would not be traded to Philadelphia, although whether this in effect negated the reserve clause was unclear. Finally, he was to be paid his salary at the start of the season, and if he were cut from the team before the season ended, he would still be entitled to the full amount. This last provision was Short's way of helping Flood out with his precarious financial situation and the uncertainties of his playing abilities after his extended absence from the game. However, Flood's early departure from the Senators while still getting his full salary would be used, as had the treble damages in his lawsuit, by his critics to bolster their claims that Flood was simply "greedy."

The return to baseball of "the Senator from Copenhagen" put Curt Flood back into the media spotlight, and his signing clearly raised a number of questions about his efforts to fight the reserve system in the courts. Even those who had supported Flood's lawsuit, such as the *New York Times*'s Leonard Koppett, wondered whether Flood would continue to pursue his case, and if he did, whether the MLBPA would continue its support. His signing also revived speculation that an out-of-court settlement of the case might be reached or that baseball owners and the association would resume serious negotiation aimed at modifying the system. Koppett raised several concerns about the possible impact of Flood's signing that Justice Goldberg may have missed or discounted when he advised Flood that a return to baseball would not preclude or jeopardize a Supreme Court ruling. For one thing, there was still the case of the American League umpires Al Salerno and Bill Valentine. At the time, their lawyer had just filed a petition for a hearing before the Supreme Court appealing the rulings against them at the district and circuit court levels. Since their case also challenged baseball's antitrust exemption, but not the reserve system, it was possible that the Supreme Court would choose to hear this case, which could, depending on their ruling, make Flood's lawsuit "academic." Another possibility was that even if Flood's attorneys and the owners agreed that his signing would not negatively influence his lawsuit, it did not guarantee or preclude the Supreme Court from taking his return into account and refusing to hear the case. As will be seen, the justices did raise the issue during oral arguments.

Flood understood that he was in for a "rough time." He knew that coming back to baseball would again make him a target for all kinds of abuse. Certainly many would call him a hypocrite or worse for claiming to fight for a principle as a "$90,000-a-year slave" and then ending up playing again for $110,000. He knew that many familiar criticisms of him as a person and a businessman would be brought up and used against him. Hadn't he originally wanted to stay in St. Louis because of his "successful" off-season business enterprises?

"Too bad," he wrote in the last pages of his memoir. "Too bad for me. Too bad for those who might misunderstand or misrepresent me." He wanted to play baseball, he needed the money, and he still believed the reserve system was wrong. After signing his contract, he returned briefly to Copenhagen to get his belongings and then traveled back to the States to once more do "my thing." Upon returning, he headed down to Florida, where, as Short had promised, he earned extra money working with the Senators' St. Petersburg farm club and began to work out in preparation for spring training. As expected, he was questioned constantly by the press, but, aside from refusing to talk about the legal aspects of his case, he attempted to be consistent, low-key, and helpful. He expressed confidence that the yearlong layoff had in fact been "good for me," and he ascribed his sojourn in another country to "mental fatigue." To reporters he appeared to be in good physical shape, and his new manager, Ted Williams, believed that Flood would prove a "great asset" to the team during the coming season. One of his teammates, slugger Frank Howard, also welcomed Flood's potential contribution to improving the Senators' record over the previous year. Just before the New Year, Flood got another piece of good news. At their winter meeting in Hawaii, the representatives of the MLBPA reaffirmed their full support of Flood's suit. According to Marvin Miller, the association wanted to "correct assumptions in the press that Flood's decision to sign with Washington had prejudiced his case and caused the players to back off in their support of his lawsuit." Miller also claimed that the owners continued to have "no interest" in resolving either the case or the reserve system issue through negotiation. This attitude was to be expected because the current Basic Agreement, approved the previous June, had in effect declared a moratorium on any such negotiations. Miller, however, hinted that some owners believed that negotiation was the best way to resolve everything.

At the end of January 1971 the appeal in *Flood v. Kuhn, et al.*, was argued before a three-judge panel of the U.S. Court of Appeals in the same Foley Square courthouse in Manhattan where the trial had taken place. The three sitting judges were Sterry R. Waterman, Leonard P. Moore, and Wilfred Feinberg. Two of the judges, Waterman and Moore, were Eisenhower appointees who had been on the appeals court for over a decade. Feinberg had been appointed to the circuit court by Lyndon Johnson in 1966 after serving on the district court in New York City for the previous five years. The oral arguments, which lasted about ninety minutes, were made by Goldberg for Flood, now the "plaintiff-appellant," and Louis Hoynes for Kuhn and the owners, now the "defendants-appellees." Both made essentially the same arguments presented in their written briefs, which themselves were based on the original filings to district court (with the exception of the fifth cause of action against the Cardinals and Yankees teams that had been dismissed by Judge Cooper). Justice Goldberg argued that the reserve clause limited a player "for life" and that all his client wanted was to be a "free man for which there is no substitute." Attorney Hoynes reminded the judges that the reserve clause had been upheld by "many" Supreme Court and lower federal court judges since 1922. The major difference in Goldberg's presentation this time was his emphasis on the second and third causes of action in the suit, those involving the applicability of state antitrust statutes to baseball. The reason for this may have been the fact that this same circuit court panel had recently ruled in the Salerno and Valentine case that baseball was exempt from federal antitrust laws.

Although a ruling by the court was anticipated within a month, a decision on Flood's appeal was not handed down for almost two more months. On April 7, 1971, the Circuit Court of Appeals announced its decision in *Flood v. Kuhn, et al.* Ironically, the decision came two days after Flood played his first regular-season professional baseball game in almost two years. Batting in his old number-two spot in the lineup, Flood got one hit and scored two runs as the Senators beat the visiting Oakland A's 8-0 in their season opener. In a unanimous decision, with one judge writing a separate concurring opinion, the circuit court upheld the lower court's ruling on all four of the causes of action. As predicted, Judges Waterman and Feinberg used their earlier ruling in the umpires' case to reaffirm *Federal Baseball* and baseball's "longstanding" and continued exemption from federal antitrust regulation. As Judge Cooper had done, the circuit court at the same time admitted that the Supreme Court's distinction between baseball and other sports was "unrealistic," "inconsistent," and "illogical." The judges cited as an example the 1957 Supreme Court ruling in *Radovich v. National Football League* in which the Court had decided that professional football was subject to the Sherman Antitrust Act.

The court then disposed of the second and third causes of action together, since both dealt with the applicability of state antitrust laws to baseball. Again, the court upheld the district court's findings in favor of the owners. But unlike Judge Cooper, the judges admitted that by so ruling, the "plaintiff is caught in a most frustrating predicament, a predicament which defendants have zealously seized upon with great perspicacity." On one hand, because of the *Federal Baseball* ruling and the principle of *stare decisis*, the plaintiff was bound to a ruling based on the conclusion that baseball was not an activity in interstate commerce. Now the plaintiff was told that "baseball is so uniquely interstate commerce that state regulation cannot apply." Of course, the judges went on to explain that this "apparent inconsistency" was not at all the result of "faulty logic" on their part but rather reflected "the vagaries of fate and this court's subordinate role to the Supreme Court." The "vagaries of fate" was a rather unusual if not perplexing rationale for judicial decision-making. How could one explain what it meant as a legal principle, if indeed it was one at all? Yet in the context of law and baseball it may have made sense, since the history of baseball is filled with fateful moments that have no easy explanation other than fate — such as why the Boston Red Sox sold Babe Ruth to the Yankees, or why Curt Flood missed that fly ball in the sixth game of the 1968 World Series. Was it the "vagaries of fate"?

By relying on their "subordinate role to the Supreme Court," Judges Waterman and Feinberg were once more using the same rationale that had appeared in almost every lower federal court ruling involving baseball since 1922. It was a variation of the legal doctrine of *stare decisis:* If courts were to follow past precedents in deciding cases, then only the Supreme Court could overturn its own precedents. Although no one had ever disputed that "subordinate role," it was not entirely clear that a lower court could under no circumstances question or come to a different conclusion about an earlier Supreme Court precedent, especially a long-standing one. What is remarkable about the Court of Appeals majority opinion in the Flood case is that while paying due deference to the conclusions of the *Federal Baseball* ruling, the judges called into question a key premise of that decision. According to Justice Holmes's opinion back in 1922, baseball was not subject to antitrust laws because it was not in interstate commerce. Now, in a footnote, the Court of Appeals urged the Supreme Court to consider "that baseball in 1971 is indeed both interstate and international commerce." The judges quoted Holmes himself to the effect that it was "revolting" to continue following a "rule of law" simply because it had been used for a long time, and it was especially wrong "if the grounds upon which it was laid down have vanished long since, and the rule simply persists from blind imitation of the past."

Whether this was a significant concession for Flood's attorneys to use when they reached the Supreme Court would have to wait. In concluding its decision, the Court of Appeals dealt with Flood's fourth cause of action in a single sentence! The judges rejected his contention that the reserve system violated the Thirteenth Amendment, "inasmuch as plaintiff retains the option not to play baseball at all." As will be seen, it was the last time the "slavery" argument would be used; Flood's attorneys would completely drop this cause of action from their Supreme Court appeal.

The opinion of Judges Waterman and Feinberg was by and large straightforward and stuck to the specific causes of action and the applicable cases and legal doctrines. The structure and operation of baseball were described with a minimum of extraneous comment or use of sports language, and when jargon was necessary, such as when they described Flood being "traded," the word was put in quotation marks and then explained, as if anyone reading the opinion would not recognize what being traded in baseball meant. Judge Moore's concurring opinion was something else again. From the opening sentence, "Baseball for almost a century has been our country's 'national' sport," it was evident that Judge Moore was more than just in "awe" of baseball — he was in love with it! Starting with "the days of Abner Doubleday and A. G. Spaulding," Judge Moore described at some length the history and "heroes" of the game as well as his own take on what had happened between the major cases to put things in "proper perspective." For example, following the 1922 *Federal Baseball* ruling, the most important development in baseball for the next thirty-one years was the fact that "the New York Yankees and Giants vied for supremacy in many of these years in World Series before huge crowds concentrating in New York from the then 48 states." (Clearly, Judge Moore did not live in Brooklyn.)

The purpose of a concurring opinion is to give a judge or justice the chance to agree with a court's findings but to disagree in his or her reasons for doing so. Judge Moore agreed "without any reservations or doubts" that all four counts of Flood's appeal should be dismissed. But his reason was simple and straightforward: Courts of law had no business getting involved in baseball. According to his reading of baseball's history over the past fifty years, organized baseball "has shown without Court interference remarkable stability under self-discipline." From *Federal Baseball* through his own court's recent ruling in *Salerno & Valentine*, Judge Moore praised this "hands off" policy. For Judge Moore, the only body that could change this situation was Congress, for only Congress had the power to "tamper" with this one particular sport that had such "national standing." Judicial restraint had been and must continue to be the court's policy. "Baseball's welfare and future should not be for the politically insulated interpreters of technical antitrust statutes but rather should be for the voters through their elected representatives." But Judge Moore's advice also carried a warning for those elected representatives who might decide to change baseball by changing the law. "If baseball is to be damaged by statutory regulation, let the congressman face his constituents the next November and also face the consequences of his baseball voting record." As for the involvement of the courts in baseball's affairs, Judge Moore would limit it solely to the chief justice, in the absence of the president, throwing out the first ball of the new baseball season.

Less than three weeks after the circuit court's ruling, Curt Flood was out of Major League Baseball for the second time. On April 27 he failed to show up at R.F.K. Stadium in D.C. for a night game with the Minnesota Twins, and the press reported that he had left that same evening from New York City's Kennedy Airport on a flight bound for Barcelona, Spain. Later it was explained that he had gotten off in Lisbon, probably en route back to Copenhagen. Why had he left this time? Afterward Flood would explain his second exit from baseball in terms of his own standards of performance on the field. Although he had started the season in promising fashion, by April 27 he had played only eight complete games in the outfield; had batted only thirty-five times; and had only a .200 batting average, all singles. He had in fact been having problems with his arm, and in the last few games he had seen action only as a pinch hitter. Yet his teammates were surprised at his departure. Infielder Elliot Maddox, Flood's roommate on road trips, explained that although he knew Flood was a "proud man" who did what he wanted, he still didn't think Flood would leave the team. First baseman Mike Epstein echoed that sentiment. He believed Flood would eventually return. "But then after I thought about it, I'm sure he won't. He's an extremely proud man."

It seems certain in hindsight that Flood's actions were indeed largely the result of his pride in his abilities and performance as a ballplayer. When it became clear, to him at least, that he was not performing up to his own standards, he left. It should also be remembered that his agreement with the Senators included the provision that if he were to be cut during the season, he was still entitled to his full salary. Because of this, he might well have decided that he should leave on his own terms rather than face the prospect that others might make that decision for him. But that is probably not the entire explanation. From the moment of his signing, he was under constant scrutiny by the press, and even those in the media who had supported him questioned the wisdom of, if not his motivation for, attempting a return to baseball. The fact that Flood's departure occurred just days after he learned that the Court of Appeals had upheld Judge Cooper's ruling on all counts was not coincidental. Mike Epstein indicated that Flood had told him that "things are closing in on me," suggesting that his playing, his ongoing legal and financial difficulties, and his latest defeat in his challenge to baseball had combined to create a situation in which Flood felt he had no alternative but to leave. There was another possible, and far more sinister, factor that explained Flood's "escape" to Europe. According to his second wife, the actress Judy Pace, Flood "thought he was going to be killed." He had received letters with threats such as "You're a dead nigger . . . we're going to kill you," and after his last game with the Senators, "there was a black wreath in his locker. A large black wreath." This was, after all, 1971 in America. April 4 had been the three-year anniversary of the assassination in Memphis of Flood's hero Martin Luther King Jr. That tragedy had been followed by bloody riots across America in which hundreds of African Americans died. The past decade had been a time of turmoil and violence in America, and calling himself a "well-paid slave" meant that Flood had to have taken such threats seriously and very personally.

The press reaction to Flood's departure from baseball merely reinforced the public image of Flood as greedy, irresponsible, and most certainly a quitter. The *St. Louis Dispatch* featured a remarkable cartoon two days after Flood's departure. It showed Flood dressed in a Spanish matador costume (although he never got as far as Spain) holding the traditional red cape in front of a charging bull. The cape was labeled "ESCAPE," and the bull carried the word "PROBLEMS" on its back. The caption evoked an understanding yet cynical view of Flood's actions. It read, "The destination of Curt Flood is said to be Spain — where he will fight the bull we all face on occasion in our lives." The drawing appeared next to a column by St. Louis sports writer Dick Young, one of Flood's earliest and most vociferous critics. He wrote that Flood had "taken off on one of his extended European tours, to the land of 'boozin and bedding.'" Young essentially accused Flood of conning Bob Short out of a lot of money for very little playing. "Flood Plays, Short Pays" read the headline of Young's column. But Young had no sympathy for Short, whom he characterized as a "sucker" for his "humanitarian" efforts to help Flood, who had then returned the favor by running off with half-a-year's salary after playing less than one-tenth of a season. Young was not alone in his hostile reaction to not only Curt Flood but Short. In fact, Flood's latest benefactor and employer had achieved an exceptional level of notoriety and infamy even before he had signed Flood. It was constantly pointed out that ever since he had come to the Senators, Short had been involved in one deal or another, including getting Bowie Kuhn to approve the hiring not only of Flood but also of McLain, who had been suspended from baseball for gambling. Short had also become notorious for his lobbying efforts in Congress to get it to lower and even eliminate the rent he had to pay to use R.F.K. Stadium. Within two years Short would become one of the most "reviled" men in Washington who was not a politician when he suddenly picked up and moved the Senators to Texas.

Much of the criticism of Flood seemed to focus more on what one fan in Denver called "another one of his escapes from reality": his money problems. His challenge to the reserve clause was usually noted but not questioned, as it had been earlier. If his return to baseball had not affected his case, why would his departure? At the end of May, Marvin Miller explained the position of the MLBPA and Flood with regard to the case and Flood's absence: "It's not the Curt Flood case against baseball. It's the reserve case and has to do with a restrictive reserve rule system which is of questionable legality. It could just as well be John Jones vs. The Owners."

CHAPTER 7

The Ex-Senator and Ex-Justice
Meet the Supreme Court

After receiving the formal notice of the Court of Appeals judgment on April 7, 1971, Flood's attorneys filed a petition on July 6, 1971, with the clerk of the U.S. Supreme Court in Washington, D.C., for a *writ of certiorari*. Having the Supreme Court grant such a writ was the first, and crucial, step in getting the Court to decide the legal and constitutional issues at stake. In effect, the petition asked the Court to grant itself jurisdiction to hear the case. This particular writ is a court order to a lower court—in this case the Court of Appeals for the Second Circuit—requiring it to produce the record of a case to the higher body for appellate review. Until the late nineteenth century, the Supreme Court had had no discretion in deciding whether or not to hear an appeal of a lower federal court ruling. In 1891 and again in 1925 Congress passed Judiciary Acts that gave the Supreme Court, except in certain cases that allowed for direct appeal to the Supreme Court, the authority to decide which cases presented significant, and new, constitutional issues that it wanted to review. Over time the custom developed that if four justices agreed that a case merited a hearing, then a *writ of certiorari* would be granted; hence the so-called Rule of Four.

Thus, it was still possible that Curt Flood's case would not be the fight to the finish that its supporters hoped for. If the Supreme Court did not accept the case, then the Court of Appeals ruling would stand, and Flood, the players, and baseball would remain frozen in their 1922 positions. With this in mind, Flood's attorneys submitted a petition that detailed the questions raised by the case and the reasons why they believed the Court should grant their petition and hear the case. The twenty-one-page petition listed five "questions presented" for the Supreme Court's ruling on:

1. Should the Supreme Court "rectify" the "bizarre result" of the Court of Appeals ruling in which the lower court had upheld the underlying idea of *Federal Baseball* that baseball was not in interstate commerce while at the same time rejecting the plaintiff's state antitrust claims on the grounds that baseball *was* in interstate commerce?

2. Had court decisions and "developments in professional sports" so undermined *Federal Baseball* and *Toolson* that they should no longer "shield" baseball's reserve system from federal antitrust laws?

3. Assuming *Federal Baseball* and *Toolson* should still stand, should baseball be exempt from state antitrust laws, thus creating "a unique 'no-man's-land' "?

4. Could the federal courts curtail the "wholesale" limitation on the applicability of state antitrust laws without a "particularized inquiry" into the specific statutes and their impact on interstate commerce?

5. Could organized baseball continue to maintain to the courts that only Congress could correct abuses of the reserve system while maintaining to Congress that the courts were "adequate and legislation unnecessary"? Also, could organized baseball continue to maintain to proponents of state regulation that federal regulation "suffices, while at the same time rejecting proponents of state regulation because of the sufficiency of federal statutes"?

In answering these questions (the first two yes and the rest no), the petition based its answers on the following "reasons":

I. The court below frankly conceded its own inability properly to dispose of this case.

II. The time has come to subject Organized Baseball's reserve system to scrutiny under the federal antitrust laws.

III. The court below ignored controlling decisions of this Court in failing to apply state antitrust law to Organized Baseball's reserve system.

IV. Organized Baseball should not be allowed to maintain, under the imprimatur of this Court, in one forum after another that "some other forum" is the appropriate one to deal with the abuses of its reserve system.

Following the submission of a response by the defendants' attorneys (including a Court-approved extension) on August 23, the Supreme Court notified both sides on October 19, 1971, that Flood's petition for a Supreme Court hearing had been granted. There is no record of which justices voted to grant *certiorari* in the case, but it is fair to assume that, given the publicity and interest that had followed the case from its inception as well as the final split decision, having at least four of the justices agree that the case should be heard had not been difficult. The case was given a docket number, No. 71-32, and a date was set by the court clerk, E. Robert Seaver, for oral arguments. Originally it was March 1, 1972, but it was later changed to March 20.

The next step was for both sides to prepare and submit their written arguments, or briefs, to the Court. Flood's attorneys Goldberg and Daniel P. Levitt submitted the brief for the "petitioner" on December 17, 1971. Goldberg had asked for a two-week extension because of other commitments. That request was denied, resubmitted, and then approved by Justice Marshall. The "respondents'" brief was submitted a month later on January 31, 1972. Considering that some briefs submitted to the Supreme Court run to hundreds of pages, both sets of briefs were relatively short and, according to one of Justice Blackmun's law clerks, well written and to the point. Both sides also submitted "reply briefs" in response to the other's original arguments. The brief on Flood's behalf followed much the same arguments and reasoning as the petition to the Supreme Court to grant *certiorari*. In effect, Flood was asking the Supreme Court to correct the mistakes of the lower courts. In the case of the trial court, it was the court's refusal, despite extensive testimony to the contrary, to make any determination on the reserve clause issue "on its merits." The Court of Appeals had then felt "compelled to affirm" that lower court ruling, even while confessing its own inability to dispose of the case on its merits. The brief highlighted Judge Waterman's admission that with respect to the federal and state antitrust issue, the appellate court's decision would leave the plaintiff in a genuine "predicament." If baseball was not subject to federal antitrust laws, and even if it was interstate commerce, then how could it at the same time be exempted from state regulation? It was now time for the Supreme Court to meet its responsibilities: "This Court is not compelled by considerations of its place in the federal judicial system to acquiesce in such an embarrassingly unsatisfactory result." Ever since 1922, organized baseball had successfully persuaded "one forum after another that 'some other forum' is the appropriate one to deal with the abuses of the reserve clause." Baseball had used Congress to get the courts to avoid dealing with the issue, then used the judiciary to get Congress to do likewise, and now baseball had added a "new" forum to the game – the "collective bargaining table and the National Labor Relations Board."

The Supreme Court brief did contain some differences from those submitted to the lower courts. One important difference was the complete elimination of the Thirteenth Amendment as an issue for consideration. The brief also described how baseball's reserve system had become "drastically more restrictive," despite owners' claims that future change in the opposite direction was inevitable. One aspect of the petitioner's argument not emphasized earlier was the problem of the effect that overruling *Federal Baseball* and *Toolson* might have on future lawsuits. The Court of Appeals had indicated its concern that overruling those two decisions would retroactively open the way for a flood of lawsuits by players who had signed contracts that contained the reserve clause going back to 1922. Citing a number of precedents in which the Supreme Court had precluded such retroactive lawsuits, Flood's brief argued that if the decisions should be overturned, it was perfectly possible for the Court to craft the decision in such a way as to provide "prospective judicial relief."

The brief submitted by Hoynes and the other lawyers representing baseball also in most respects mirrored the earlier submissions to the district court and Court of Appeals. Naturally, the "respondents" took advantage of the favorable opinions in both lower courts by citing them throughout, and it certainly didn't hurt that the lower courts had ruled in baseball's favor on all of the causes of action. Much of the brief was devoted to a historical, economic, and legal defense of the reserve system and its significance as the "cornerstone of the present structure" of the game. The reserve system, it argued, had been and was responsible for everything that had made professional baseball so popular and so successful over the years. The system maintained the competitive balance between the teams and the public's confidence in the integrity of the game. It was also necessary to support the high costs of new player development and maintain the benefits to all, including the players, of the "economic stability" that resulted from the system. Contrary to the petitioners' claim that baseball's system was more "restrictive" than those of other sports, the brief claimed that differences between the sports were "slight and more cosmetic than real."

From the commissioner's and owners' perspective, the mandatory collective bargaining process set up with the Major League Baseball Players Association provided the most logical avenue to consider changes in the reserve system. In the owners' version, the reserve system was already a subject of meaningful and constructive negotiation between them and the association. However, despite progress, the association had become "impatient" and "eager to obtain the assistance of the federal courts to bend the clubs to their demands," resulting in the current lawsuit. In fact, this lawsuit was "a perversion of the antitrust laws" and an "obvious effort" of the association to gain added "leverage" in the collective bargaining process. The brief rebutted association claims that the bargaining process had proven unproductive and that the players were too "weak" to get the owners to seriously negotiate the issue. Of course, it also pointed out that both Judge Cooper and the Court of Appeals judges had endorsed collective bargaining as the reasonable solution. Conceding that the reserve system was "evolving" and its modification was "possible — even likely," it predicted that attempts to bring about such changes through antitrust litigation, such as this case, could only produce "harrassment [*sic*] and disruption."

The second half of the brief focused on case law and "sound reasons" to continue "adherence to the long unbroken line of precedent in this Court holding that Baseball's reserve system" is not subject to either federal or state antitrust laws and is not exempt from federal labor policies requiring collective bargaining to settle "labor-management" disputes. The earlier baseball rulings needed to be upheld because the current structure and future development of baseball were based on owners' and potential owners' "reliance" on these decisions and the reserve system. The validity of this idea would be one of the main issues debated by both sides in their "reply briefs." Essentially, "reliance" is the other side of *stare decisis:* Courts and judges should follow precedents because people (and lawyers) rely on such continuity in making future decisions, especially economic ones.

In a lawsuit that had seen its small moments of drama, the oral arguments before the Supreme Court on March 20, 1972, would certainly have made the highlights film. It would be one of the very few instances in modern times that a former Supreme Court justice would appear on the other side of the bench to argue a case before his former colleagues (the other being, ironically, Goldberg's replacement on the Court, Abe Fortas). Justice Goldberg had been appointed to the Court in 1962 by President Kennedy. But after Goldberg had served only three terms on the Court, President Lyndon Johnson had convinced him to take over as U.S. ambassador to the United Nations. After several frustrating years at the UN, Goldberg had resigned and returned to private practice, becoming a partner in the New York City law firm Paul, Weiss, Goldberg, Rifkind, Wharton & Garrison. After his defeat in the 1970 New York gubernatorial contest, Goldberg had left that firm and set up a law office in Washington, D.C.

Missing that day in the courtroom was the plaintiff himself. Curt Flood had left for Europe in April 1971 and, according to one account, was working in Spain as a sportscaster for an English-language radio station. Also appearing was Levitt, an attorney with Goldberg's New York firm. Appearing for the respondents were Paul A. Porter of the Washington, D.C., law firm Arnold & Porter and Louis L. Hoynes, who had represented the defendants from the trial onward. Hoynes had recently been appointed chief counsel for the National League. Under Court rules, each side would be allowed thirty minutes to make its presentations, and usually that was done by one attorney for each side. However, just before the hearing the Court approved a request by the respondents that Porter take five minutes to speak on behalf of Bowie Kuhn, as commissioner of baseball, with Hoynes following on behalf of the owners.

The Supreme Court in March 1972 was a court in transition. The nine justices were a mixed bag, split between newer Republican presidential appointees and longer-serving Democratic appointees. The chief justice, Warren E. Burger, had been chosen by recently elected President Richard M. Nixon in 1969 following the retirement of liberal icon Chief Justice Earl Warren. A judge of the Court of Appeals for the District of Columbia at the time of his elevation, Burger was viewed as a moderate conservative who had shown himself to be the kind of tough judge who reflected Nixon's 1968 "law and order" presidential campaign theme. Associate Justice Harry M. Blackmun, a fellow Minnesotan and friend of Burger, was Nixon's second appointee. Blackmun's nomination came after Nixon's first three choices, all Southerners, had been rejected by the Senate. Blackmun filled the seat vacated by Justice Abe Fortas, who had resigned after only four years on the Court because of a conflict-of-interest scandal. During his first years on the Court, Blackmun would so often be on the same side of a case as the chief justice that the press dubbed them the "Minnesota Twins." The two newest justices were Lewis F. Powell Jr. and William Rehnquist. Powell, a Richmond, Virginia, attorney and former president of the American Bar Association, was appointed to fill Justice Hugo Black's seat on the Court. At least early on, Justice Powell leaned toward the moderate center and tended to avoid doctrinal extremes. He also tended to follow precedents, even those he may have originally disagreed with. At the time of his nomination in 1972 (he and Powell were confirmed a few days apart), William H. Rehnquist was assistant U.S. attorney general. More than Powell, Rehnquist came to the Court with a reputation as a hard-line conservative. He proved true to his reputation. Two of the justices were President Dwight D. Eisenhower appointees from the 1950s: Potter Stewart (1958) and William Brennan (1956). In the years since their appointment, Stewart had tended to become more of a moderate on the bench, whereas Brennan had become one of the Court's most consistent liberals. Justice Byron R. White was one of two Supreme Court appointees of President John F. Kennedy, the other being Arthur Goldberg. Although he also began his career with a reputation as a liberal, White often sided with the moderate Stewart. The rest of the Court consisted of William O. Douglas, the longest-serving justice, appointed by President Franklin D. Roosevelt in 1939, and the first African American Supreme Court justice, Thurgood Marshall, appointed by President Lyndon Johnson in 1967. Marshall had been appointed after a distinguished career as an attorney for the Legal Defense Fund of the National Association for the Advancement of Colored People (NAACP). Marshall and the fund had been responsible for legal challenges against racial segregation and discrimination from World War II to the 1960s. Stewart and White had thus far tended to be "centrists" in their judicial leanings, whereas Douglas, Brennan, and Marshall were generally found on the liberal end of the Court's decisions.

Even before the oral arguments began on March 20, a "bit of a problem" arose. How, the justices wondered, was their former colleague to be addressed in court? In earlier correspondence, the Supreme Court's clerk had headed letters to "Mr. Justice Goldberg." But in the official transcript of the oral arguments on March 20, Goldberg was referred to as "Mr. Goldberg," and when the justices began asking him questions, they too referred to him as "Mr. Goldberg." Beginning his presentation with the traditional opening, "Mr. Chief Justice, and may it please the Court . . ." Goldberg went on to outline the basic issues in the case, including an explanation of the reserve system and a detailed account of how Curt Flood had come to sue baseball (he got a minor fact wrong — according to Goldberg, Flood had received the form notice of his trade before the phone call). Goldberg's presentation was less than impressive, and reporters Bob Woodward and Scott Armstrong claimed that Goldberg's former colleagues on the Court were in fact "embarrassed" by his performance. Justice Blackmun thought the ex-justice seemed "troubled," and Goldberg admitted to Justice Blackmun afterward that it had probably been a mistake for him to appear before his former colleagues. It is not unusual for the justices to break into an oral argument rather quickly with questions, since they are presumably familiar with the case, having read the records and briefs beforehand. In this instance, they let Goldberg go on for quite a while, and when they did ask questions, they concerned relatively minor points or details, such as the salary offered to Flood by Philadelphia. At one point, when he indicated that he was about to move on to another issue, Goldberg was interrupted by Chief Justice Burger, who said, "I hope you're going to get to that; you're talking rather . . ." Goldberg replied, "I will move fast." Evidently he did not move fast enough because he was still getting to yet another issue when the chief justice informed him that his time was "completely consumed." However, he was granted an extra three minutes.

Aside from the mention of several recent labor cases, almost everything Goldberg started to discuss (since he often did not finish particular points) repeated arguments presented in the briefs and in the petition for *certiorari*. As Justice Blackmun remembered it, Goldberg seemed more intent on lecturing his former colleagues than on presenting arguments or highlighting certain aspects of the case that would convince the Court to rule in favor of his client. As a result, many of the exchanges between Goldberg and the justices made the courtroom sound more like a college lecture hall. Goldberg appeared more comfortable displaying his expertise, especially with regard to labor law, than in convincing the Court to overturn a long-standing position. He had either forgotten or not realized that the question of the reserve system and the Thirteenth Amendment was no longer part of his case, since he referred to it as one of the issues before the Court. He also spent a good deal of time trying to explain exactly what damages Curt Flood had suffered by not signing with Philadelphia. He conceded that Flood would have to have signed with some other team once the Cardinals had made it known that they didn't want him. That Goldberg described Flood's desire to be a "free agent" as meaning that he could make his "own deal" implied that Flood was more concerned with money than with a principle. He made things even more confusing when he stated that Flood had "left" baseball. "Is the case moot, therefore?" he was asked. Goldberg replied that it wasn't because of the 1970 season. But he went on to say that Flood had returned "later," and that he had the "right to decide if he want[ed] to go to the minor leagues or Japan, which are subject to the same rules." Fortunately for the former justice, he was at that point informed that his time had expired.

If the number and quality of questions asked by the justices during oral arguments are indicative of the quality of the arguments presented by the attorneys, then it was the two attorneys for baseball who outscored their opponent. Paul Porter, speaking first on behalf of Commissioner Kuhn, focused on explaining the role of the commissioner, who Porter claimed occupied a "neutral position" in the relationship between the players and the owners. In this position, the commissioner was responsible for ensuring the "continuity of employment" of players and the "honesty of the sport" by ensuring equality of competition. According to Porter, this case was essentially a labor dispute that Commissioner Kuhn had testified was in fact being looked at through the "bargaining process" at the time that "this litigation was brought by the players union." This statement prompted an interesting exchange:

Question: But, Mr. Porter, you just said when this litigation was
   brought by the players union?

Mr. Porter: Oh, it was financed by the players union, indeed that's
   conceded in this record. . . .

Question: Are you saying this is their lawsuit, not Flood's?

Mr. Porter: Absolutely, yes, sir.

As Marvin Miller's earlier comment after the trial had implied, it
appeared that except in name and symbolically, Curt Flood was dis-
appearing from his own case. What Porter suggested, Louis Hoynes,
who followed him on behalf of the National League, elaborated on
and confirmed. Both Porter and Hoynes argued that the record of the
case showed that the reserve system had already been made a "mandatory" subject of collective bargaining between the owners and the
players' union and that both sides were already considering possible
changes. Hoynes reminded the justices that during the trial, Flood's
testimony had been "isolated" from that of the other witnesses on his
behalf. Flood had wanted the "entire system torn apart," whereas the
other witnesses had limited their testimony to supporting "modifications" in the system, which they agreed in fact were "necessary." "This
testimony," Hoynes concluded, "represented a repudiation, really, of
Mr. Flood's position, and left him the forgotten man for the remain-
der of the case. In fact, no evidence at all was offered on the damages
which Mr. Flood's complaint indicated he had suffered."

Unlike Goldberg, Hoynes appeared relaxed and confident during
his presentation. As the justices peppered him with questions from
the start, he was able to focus on the issues and make the points he
wanted, even prompting the only instances of laughter during the hour
of oral arguments. Much of his argument focused on the reserve
clause, or "system," as he explained it, and how it was necessary for
baseball. When questioned about how other sports managed to get
along without the reserve system, Hoynes explained how baseball's
reliance on minor leagues for developing players made the sport
unique, and he pointed out that even without the reserve system, football and basketball players complained that their freedom of movement between teams was too restricted. The one time that Hoynes
seemed to get flustered occurred when he cited a recently published
law review article that he claimed supported his argument that

antitrust issues were "irrelevant" in this case and that this case was a matter of labor policy to be decided through collective bargaining. Asked if he thought, therefore, that the case should be sent back to the lower courts to determine the labor exemption issue "on its merits," Hoynes had to admit that it would "not be inappropriate." He concluded his presentation by reminding the justices that under the doctrine of *stare decisis*, they were obligated to uphold *Federal Baseball* and *Toolson*. For good measure, he once more pointed out that if any change in policy was needed "then Congress, as this Court has repeatedly observed, is the proper body for adopting that."

It was expected that once oral arguments had been heard, the Supreme Court would announce its decision within a matter of weeks, but as it turned out, it was almost two months before the decision was announced. Following oral arguments, the next step in the judicial process was for the justices to meet in conference to discuss the case and take an initial vote. In the past, these conferences had been scheduled at different times, but since he had become chief justice, Burger had favored Wednesday and Friday afternoons. However, with important cases, or to deal with a backlog of cases, the Court would meet at other times. These conferences are secret, and no one other than the justices are permitted in the conference room while they are deliberating. No official record is kept of what is said, and once a vote is taken, the chief justice (or the senior justice if the chief justice is in the minority) assigns someone to draft the majority opinion. However, some justices over the years have taken their own notes on these discussions, and thanks to Justices Douglas and Brennan, there was a record of the conference and the initial vote in *Flood v. Kuhn*. The conference was held on Monday afternoon, the same day as oral arguments. During these conferences there is also a long-standing tradition for the justices to speak and vote in order of their seniority following the chief justice. Chief Justice Burger began by indicating that "*Toolson* is probably wrong," suggesting that he would vote to reverse the Court of Appeals and trial decisions. Justice Douglas likewise voted to reverse and remand the case back to the district court for a new trial. Douglas stated that baseball should be treated the same as football and basketball. He also agreed that *Toolson* was "out of our 'stream of commerce' decisions" and should therefore be treated as an antitrust case. Justice Brennan, who had dissented in the *Radovich* case, now also agreed that *Toolson* should be overruled. However, Brennan also noted that the labor exemption issue had not been addressed in *Toolson;* therefore, he would send the case back to the lower court for a new trial to deal with that issue. Brennan agreed that state antitrust laws did not apply, and although he conceded that the reserve clause "may have certain advantages," it was not an issue on which the Court needed to decide.

Justice Potter Stewart voted to affirm the lower courts' rulings. Stewart's position was straightforward: Congress had "explicitly" exempted baseball from antitrust laws, and by implication from state regulation as well. Its exemption was not "inadvertent," and therefore Stewart would "leave it to Congress to decide." Justices White and Marshall both agreed with Stewart to affirm. Justice Blackmun indicated that he would likewise affirm, but "tentatively." He saw the case as more of a labor dispute than an antitrust case. "Baseball was a sport, not a business," he stated. "Today it is a business." Justice Powell then announced to his colleagues that because of his stock ownership in the Anheuser-Busch Company (which owned the Cardinals), he would not be taking part in the decision. He would, in judicial terms, recuse himself. However, he went on to explain that in his view the lower courts' decisions should be reversed. His argument was as straightforward as Stewart's, for the opposite reason. For Justice Powell it made "no sense" that baseball should be treated any differently than football. He concluded, "Congressional inaction only means that they won't act unless we force them to by reversing. Congress is apt to be mute as long as we have solved the problem for them." The newest justice, Rehnquist, also voted to affirm. But although he agreed with Stewart that "*Toolson* had crossed the bridge," Rehnquist was less certain that state antitrust laws might apply, and he indicated that he "might" be willing to send the case back down on that issue. Finally the chief justice indicated his intention by simply stating, "I reverse."

Thus, as of March 24, there appeared to be a majority (Stewart, White, Marshall, Blackmun, and Rehnquist) of votes to affirm the lower courts' ruling against Curt Flood. But such a count included two tentative supporters (Blackmun and Rehnquist) and one recusant (Powell), who indicated that he would have voted in favor of Flood. Once the vote was taken, one of the justices in the majority, Justice Blackmun, was assigned to draft an opinion that would then be circulated among the other justices. Normally this assignment would have been made by the chief justice, but since Burger had not voted with the majority, the assigning fell to the next in seniority, Justice Stewart. Once circulated, the opinion would be revised and criticized, and if necessary, other justices could write concurring or dissenting opinions. Like the conference, this part of the process of Supreme Court decision-making is and has been kept from the public eye and the historical record. However, in 1979 Bob Woodward (of Watergate fame) and Scott Armstrong published their "behind-the-scenes" account of the Supreme Court from 1969 to 1975: *The Brethren: Inside The Supreme Court*. Based on extensive interviews, mainly with the justices' law clerks, Court employees, and "several Justices," the book quickly became a best seller as it showed how much the personalities, alliances, feuds, and foibles of the individual justices and their staffs shaped the decisions of the nation's highest judicial body. One of the cases used to demonstrate this was *Flood v. Kuhn*, and according to Woodward and Armstrong, the final decision was the result of several weeks of negotiation, switching sides, and implied "vote-trading." Because they based their description of how the Court reached its decision on uncited sources, it is difficult to confirm the accuracy of their account. However, in a 1980 letter to Daniel Crystal, an associate editor of the Passaic County Bar Association's journal *The Reporter*, Justice Blackmun wrote that "the Woodward-Armstrong references to *Flood v. Kuhn* and its development were kind enough but embrace more than one factual error."

The Supreme Court's decision in *Flood v. Kuhn* was announced on June 19, 1972, both parties being notified by telegram. In a 5-3 ruling the Court affirmed the Court of Appeals and district court rulings against Flood on all causes of action. However, the makeup of the majority was different than it had first appeared at the conference vote in March. The majority now consisted of Justices Blackmun, Stewart, Rehnquist, Burger, and White, with both White and Burger separately indicating their concurrence in Blackmun's opinion, except for Part 1. Indeed, it was Part 1 of Justice Blackmun's opinion in *Flood v. Kuhn* that would elicit much of the commentary and criticism on the decision. Part 1, titled "The Game," was a brief history of baseball that included a list of names of ballplayers "celebrated for one reason or another, that have sparked the diamond and its environs and that have provided tinder for recaptured thrills . . . and for conversation and anticipation in-season and off season." What was so remarkable was that the list included more than *eighty* names, or almost an entire page in the official reports. The "list" included players that most people would have easily recognized, such as Babe Ruth, Ty Cobb, and Lou Gehrig. But it also included a good number of names of ballplayers, such as Heinie Groh, Big Dan Brothers, and Chief Bender, that even the most die-hard baseball fans in 1972 would have been hard-pressed to recall. Woodward and Armstrong believed that this unusual beginning may have played a role in Justice Marshall's switching his vote and ending up writing a separate dissent. They believed Marshall had become upset when the original version of the list had been circulated because it contained no names of African American players. In later years Blackmun denied this, citing it as example of one of the reporters' errors. Blackmun claimed that as a boy he remembered Roy Campanella playing for the Dodgers' minor league farm club, so Campanella would have to have been on the original list (along with Satchel Paige and Jackie Robinson). Blackmun admitted that he had left one obvious great player off the list — Mel Ott. The first part concluded with a number of literary references to baseball, including the famous poem "Casey at the Bat."

Justice Blackmun always referred to this section as my "short sentimental journey" into baseball and was "disappointed" that instead of the *per curium* opinion he originally drafted that would represent the entire majority, Chief Justice Burger and Justice White ended up stating that they concurred with the Court's opinion "in all but Part I." The chief justice had switched his vote, but why he did so is not clear. In a memo to Blackmun several weeks after Blackmun had begun circulating the draft of his opinion, Burger stated, "After much travail I come out on this case as a 'reluctant affirm.'" The remaining five parts of *Flood v. Kuhn* were neither surprising nor novel except for the additional citations from the Court of Appeal's ruling to support the decision. Organized baseball's reserve system had enjoyed exemption from federal antitrust legislation since *Federal Baseball*, and that exemption had been confirmed by *Toolson*. This exemption, even though an "aberration" as well as "unrealistic, inconsistent, or illogical," was one of long standing and therefore "entitled to the benefits of *stare decisis.*" Even though the courts had expanded the concept of interstate commerce, it was clear that professional baseball was "a business and it is engaged in interstate commerce." In a footnote, Justice Blackmun, though noting that *Federal Baseball* was not one of Holmes's "happier days," still defended that opinion on one point. Contrary to "what many believe," Holmes had recognized baseball as a business. Still, Justice Blackmun once more concluded that "baseball's unique characteristics and needs" required the continuation of that special exemption. The Court also concluded that Congress "as yet has had no intention" to change baseball's status, even as the majority's "preference" was for any change to come from the legislature. Justice Blackmun presented an interesting reason for this preference that the Court of Appeals had only indirectly alluded to. A Court ruling overturning *Federal Baseball* and *Toolson* would inevitably result in "confusion and the retroactivity problems," whereas if Congress made the change by passing a law, such a law would only be "prospective in operation." In other words if the Supreme Court did overrule *Federal Baseball*, there would be, as the Court of Appeals had predicted, a "flood of litigation" in addition to Curt Flood's.

Justice Blackmun and the majority also had "a word" about Flood's claim that state antitrust laws might apply to baseball's reserve clause. Such laws were not relevant, despite baseball's own "inconsistent position" in the past on this issue. The Court also found it "unnecessary" to deal with the related cause of action and simply noted baseball's argument that the reserve system was a subject for collective bargaining and that federal labor laws therefore "exempt" the reserve system from federal antitrust laws. As if to make sure of the point, the Court concluded its opinion using a quotation from the concluding lines of *Toolson*. And "what the Court said in *Federal Baseball* in 1922, and what it said in *Toolson* in 1953, we say again here in 1972: the remedy, if any is indicated, is for congressional and not judicial action." As noted earlier, Justice White separately concurred with the opinion "in all but Part I," doing so after Blackmun had rejected White's "gentle suggestion" to omit that section. Chief Justice Burger filed a separate one-paragraph concurrence, which also excluded Part 1. The chief justice admitted his "grave reservations" about the correctness of *Toolson* but agreed that the courts were not the forum "in which this tangled web ought to be unsnarled." Even if it was "the least undesirable course," it was time that Congress acted to solve the problem.

There were two dissenting opinions in the case. The first, written by Justice Douglas with Justice Brennan concurring, zeroed in on *Federal Baseball*, calling it a "derelict in the stream of the law that we, its creator, should remove." The use of the phrase "stream of the law" was both intentional and ironic, reflecting Douglas's New Deal roots and the impact of the New Deal on the expansion of the "stream of commerce" principle with regard to federal regulation of interstate commerce. For Douglas, it was clear that baseball "is today big business that is packaged with beer, with broadcasting, and with other industries." Whatever the situation may have been in 1922, baseball was now part of interstate commerce and therefore subject to congressional regulation. Moreover, *Federal Baseball* was unfair: Its "beneficiaries" were "not the Babe Ruths, Ty Cobbs, and Lou Gehrigs," and the owners had a "proclivity for predatory practices." Douglas also argued that congressional inaction was no excuse for the Court not to protect the "victims" of an unreasonable restraint of trade prohibited by the Sherman Act. Justice Douglas concluded his dissent with an unusual admission: "While I joined the Court's opinion in *Toolson v. New York* . . . I have lived to regret it; and I would now correct what I believe to be its fundamental error."

The second dissent was written by Justice Marshall, with Brennan concurring. As noted before, Marshall had originally voted in the conference to affirm the lower courts' rulings against Flood. At the March 20 conference, Marshall had indicated his vote after Potter Stewart had voted to affirm based on the single issue of Congress's exemption of baseball from antitrust laws. Marshall had stated, "I agree with Potter and vote to affirm." It was after Justice Blackmun circulated his first draft of the majority opinion that Marshall drafted his own opinion and circulated it to the other justices. The Woodward-Armstrong book claimed Marshall's "switch" had to do with Blackmun's exclusion of African American stars from his "list." In actuality, Justice Marshall's dissent was not that much of a switch. What made his opinion remarkable was that from the start he had focused on the "forgotten man," Curt Flood, and the reserve system. Since the issue of the reserve system and the Thirteenth Amendment had not been raised by Flood's attorneys, Justice Marshall came as close as anyone on the Court to bringing it back, or at least referring to it, if indirectly. In explaining why Flood had brought this case in the first place, Marshall stated, "To non-athletes it might appear that petitioner [Flood] was virtually enslaved by the owners of major league baseball clubs who bartered among themselves for his services. But athletes know that it was not servitude that bound petitioner to the club owners; it was the reserve system."

It was this system that *Federal Baseball* and *Toolson* had allowed to go unchecked by federal laws for so long, and for Marshall, that situation was simply unfair. He recognized that this case was "difficult" because it presented a choice between the important principle of *stare decisis* and following decisions that were "totally at odds with more recent and better reasoned cases." But for Justice Marshall, the more important principle at stake was the Supreme Court's role in the protection of "substantial federal rights." In this instance, it was the right of all citizens, whether they be baseball players, "football players, lawyers, doctors, or members of any other class of workers," to have the protection of antitrust laws and the ability to compete "freely and effectively to the best of one's ability." Marshall was also confident that the Court could have crafted a decision overruling the two earlier cases without making the decision retroactive.

The final section of Marshall's dissent suggested that he had changed his vote not simply because Blackmun's opinion had left out African American baseball stars. Rather, he had come to believe that as a result of *Federal Baseball* and *Toolson*, "some 600 baseball players" had been left out, as it were, and deprived of their right to compete freely under the protection of the antitrust laws. What "muscle" the baseball players might have been able to "muster" by combining with athletes from other sports "has been greatly impaired by the manner in which this Court has isolated them. It is this Court which has made them impotent, and this Court should correct its error." By this reasoning, baseball players had become an example of the kind of "separate and unequal" status that Justice Marshall's entire life and career on the bench had been dedicated to eliminating.

Justice Marshall had clearly switched his position on the question of overturning *Federal Baseball* and *Toolson*. But he qualified the possible outcome if the Court had done so, explaining that even if these decisions were overruled, Flood would not necessarily "prevail." The reason for this was a "hurdle of recent vintage" that Flood would have had to overcome at a new trial. That hurdle was the collective bargaining agreement set up by the owners and the MLBPA seven years earlier. In Marshall's opinion, the exact nature of the "collective bargaining relationship" had not been fully "explored" either at the district court trial or in the Court of Appeals appellate ruling. It appears that he was not persuaded, at least from the record, that the reserve clause was either a subject of labor-management relations subject to federal labor policies — that is, the National Labor Relations Board process (respondents' position) — or a provision of the agreement "thrust" upon the players by the owners that violated antitrust laws (petitioner's position). The solution for Marshall would be to send the case back for "consideration" of whether, despite the collective bargaining agreement, Flood could prove his antitrust claims. That would have brought the case back to where it had started, since it could not happen unless the court also overturned baseball's exemption from those same antitrust laws. Since Justice Marshall had voted to affirm based on Justice Stewart's view of the case as one involving the simple issue of a congressional exemption from antitrust laws, it is possible that Blackmun's opinion might have seemed to him like judicial overkill, especially with its obvious bias toward the owners' view of what was in the "best interests" of the game. Marshall took seriously the motto over the entrance to the Supreme Court building that the Court was there to provide "equal justice for all." Blackmun's opinion, with or without the list, may have prompted Marshal to reconsider his initial vote.

As noted before, the Supreme Court's decision in *Flood v. Kuhn* indicated that Justice Lewis Powell "took no part in the consideration or decision of the case." The day after oral arguments, Justice Powell had sent a memo to his colleagues confirming the "fact" that the St. Louis Cardinals were owned by a subsidiary of Anheuser-Busch. Despite the efforts of his clerks and others to convince him otherwise, Justice Powell continued to maintain that because of his ownership of Busch stock, his participation would be a conflict of interest. Although he indicated that he would have voted against the company, he also believed that his vote would not have changed the outcome.

CHAPTER 8

"Flood Strikes Out"

At least two experts had gotten it wrong. Harold Spaeth, a Michigan State University political scientist and a pioneer in using computer analyses of the Supreme Court (this was 1972), predicted that Curt Flood would win. He also predicted that the vote would be unanimous, although it was possible that Justice Rehnquist might dissent. Washington, D.C., sportswriter Tom Dowling was convinced that baseball would lose and *Toolson* would be overruled. His methods were less scientific than Spaeth's: Dowling had merely sat through the oral arguments before the Supreme Court and then analyzed the "pitchers" on both sides. Lou Hoynes had shown "good stuff" as the "pitcher of record" for baseball, whereas Goldberg had taken so long to "wind up" that by the time he had thrown his first pitch, his half-hour "inning" (and three extra minutes) had been up, leaving his ball hanging "indefinitely in midair." Despite the unequal match-up, Dowling concluded that "no one seriously expects the court to go down swinging once again on baseball's pitch." He thought it most likely that Flood's case would be remanded, Flood would end up with a "bundle" of money, and Bowie Kuhn would have to start talking with the players about free agency.

Others' reactions to the Supreme Court's ruling in the Flood case took much the same approach as Dowling's, converging bench and ball field. The *New York Daily News*, for example, reported that "baseball won its legal World Series today. The score was 5-3." Its explanation of the decision was headlined, "Flood Strikes Out in Supreme Court." Other newspapers and sports magazines reported the decision, and, as the *Sporting News* noted, "everybody has [an] opinion," whether or not they agreed with the Court's majority. Tom Dowling thought the ruling "astounding" and believed that even by the most "charitable interpretation," it showed that the Court had not considered the "clear if lucrative servitude of ballplayers as a very serious public issue." It was not, Dowling wrote, "the court's finest hour." Others in the press and media who had supported Flood were likewise surprised by the decision and certainly astonished by Justice Blackmun's opinion. Bill Veeck, who had testified on Flood's behalf at the trial, acknowledged that he was "shaken" by the decision and called Blackmun's opinion "weird." Veeck wished that Justice Blackmun had shown the same "diligence" and respect for the law as he had shown for baseball in his opening section and listing of the game's great players.

From the beginning of the lawsuit, Leonard Koppett of the *New York Times* had consistently supported Flood. He believed that baseball's arguments as the case made its way through the legal system were generally "pathetic." Yet in his stories and columns, he had done as much as anyone to fairly and plainly describe the issues involved and what was happening at each step of the case. Koppett was not all that surprised at the outcome, mainly because he saw the lawsuit as only one battle in a larger campaign. Indeed, he believed the decision had achieved some positive results. For one thing, the Supreme Court had refused to put its "seal of approval" on the reserve system, and by its use of "tortured logic" the Court had called attention to the absurdity of baseball's position. Moreover, the players, provided that they now truly organized, still had the possibility of changing the system through the bargaining process, making "their next pitch to Congress." That was the more effective strategy, in Koppett's view. Marvin Miller likewise thought the Flood decision had "no internal logic" and Justice Blackmun's opinion was rather undignified. However, Miller could also look on the positive side. "A lot has happened in the last two years," he stated, "[and] the climate now is much more favorable for negotiation." Like Koppett, the director of the players' association tried to look at the case as a "catalyst for change" and believed that "constructive results now are quite possible through negotiation." Such sentiments were echoed by Commissioner Kuhn, who recalled that "far from claiming victory, I was espousing collective bargaining as the road for change in the reserve system. The last thing I wanted was the clubs to view the Flood decision as an excuse for doing nothing. Change was in the wind." Although the editorial page of the *Min-*

neapolis Tribune, Blackmun's hometown, found the decision "puzzling," it too hoped that now the players and owners could reach agreement through the bargaining process.

Inevitably, reaction to the case raised the question of why Flood and the players had lost. Especially "annoying" to Miller and the others directly involved in the case was the charge that Flood had somehow sold the Major League Baseball Players Association a "bill of goods" and that they could have picked a more sympathetic case to support than Flood's — that is, an instance of a less-well-paid player. Miller's response at the time and later was to simply remind everyone that "Flood is probably the only real loser in this case" and that eventually the players would benefit and the reserve system would be changed. He rejected the notion that Flood, being the highly paid player that he was at the time, was the wrong choice, pointing to the earlier example of the more "fringe" player George Toolson, who had also lost. Miller also pointed out that even had Flood "won," the case would likely have been remanded to the lower courts for further litigation.

As described in Chapter 5, Miller had admitted several of his own mistakes that he felt might have made a difference, at least during the trial. One of these, the lack of more public support and participation of the active players who made up the association, was certainly true. Both the briefs and oral arguments of the owners alluded to the fact that only one active player had testified on Flood's behalf during the trial. But whether this absence affected the Supreme Court's decision-making as much as it probably did the impressionable and star-struck Judge Cooper is unclear. The other error Miller acknowledged was getting Arthur Goldberg to represent Flood. At the time that Miller had first approached the former justice, Goldberg had assured him that, contrary to rumors going around, he had no intention of entering politics as the New York Democratic Party's gubernatorial candidate in the 1970 elections. In fact, Goldberg did run, yet proved to be such an "underwhelming campaigner" that he managed to turn an early lead in the polls into one of the most lopsided defeats in modern state history, giving incumbent Nelson Rockefeller a fourth term by more than 600,000 votes. Miller felt "betrayed," having "underestimated the allure of political office even to a man like Goldberg." Following the election Goldberg left his New York firm, to the relief of his colleagues, it seems, and set up his own office in Washington, D.C.

But he insisted on continuing with the case, and, as even the sports-writer Dowling recognized, his performance during oral arguments only confirmed Miller's and others' judgment that having the former justice represent Flood and the players had been a "bad call."

Much of the "postgame" analyses of the Supreme Court's ruling focused on Blackmun's unusual and unique opinion, particularly the opening section (it turned out he had done a similar "historical" opening in a case involving Native Americans). After Woodward and Armstrong's book *The Brethren* appeared, the internal politics and personalities of the other justices on the Court were highlighted. The implication of "vote-trading" among the justices (possibly Burger and Blackmun) added a touch of conspiracy to the story as well as further confirming in the public's mind the notion that the Supreme Court was no different or more "honorable" than any other institution or branch of government. Even Marvin Miller cautiously accepted this explanation for the case's outcome, expressing his amazement at how close Flood and the players had actually come to winning the case. Bill Veeck added his own contribution to the story by repeating a "well-traveled" rumor about Justice White, who had been known as "Whizzer" during his years as an all-American college football player and afterward in a brief professional football career. White had voted against his fellow athletes because he was trying to burnish his "moderate" credentials for the upcoming Democratic Party presidential nominating convention.

The Flood decision was also seen in broader political terms as evidence of the growing reaction against the "liberalism" of Supreme Court decisions, especially during Chief Justice Earl Warren's tenure from 1953 to 1968. The elements of this liberalism included an activist judiciary willing to promote equality and, by interpreting the Constitution broadly, to uphold federal authority over the protection of civil rights for minorities as well as individual rights and liberties as defined by the Bill of Rights. Republican president Nixon's election in 1968 marked the beginning of a "revival of conservative constitutionalism" insofar as his judicial appointees were almost always Republicans who reflected the opposite characteristics of liberalism. These judges favored "judicial restraint," the notion that courts should generally defer to the wishes of the legislature. Conservatives supported the rolling back of federal programs and rights protections while enhancing the role and responsibilities of the states. On the nine-member Supreme Court, there was also a third category: "moderate" or "centrist" justices who played an important role as the "swing" votes in close or controversial cases. From this perspective, *Flood v. Kuhn* certainly reflected the increasingly visible conservative-liberal divide on the Supreme Court. Four of the five justices on the majority side (Blackmun, Burger, Rehnquist, and Stewart) had been Republican and all three dissenters (Douglas, Brennan, and Marshall) were Democratic appointees. There was also Justice White, who sided with the conservatives, although a Democrat (and ex-athlete himself). Justice Powell, a Republican, had removed himself from the decision. But had he voted, he would have sided with "liberals" in favor of Flood, which would have resulted in a case of judicial swinging both ways. The same holds true for Chief Justice Burger and Justice Marshall, both of whom also ended up switching their votes. But in their case it was a change back to their regular doctrinal positions.

The public's reaction to *Flood v. Kuhn* and its understanding of the case in terms of Blackmun's opinion or the Court's personalities and behavioral politics was only part of the story. After 1972, references to and analyses of the decision appeared in a growing number of law reviews and scholarly journals as well as textbooks and treatises on sports, antitrust, and labor law. For the most part, these were critical of the decision for a variety of jurisprudential reasons: the rigidity of the Court's reliance on *stare decisis*, the deference given to legislative inaction rather than the normal "judicial restraint" position of deference to legislative action, and, the incongruity of a decision denying both federal and state application of antitrust statutes. For those involved in the nascent but expanding legal subfield of "sports law," the case became the prime example of how a particular professional sport could maintain its privileged legal status by self-reference to its unique status as a "national pastime." Baseball's antitrust "anomaly" became the legal exception that illustrated the rule (which also explains why the case continues to appear in sports and labor law casebooks).

By the 1980s and early 1990s, it became increasingly difficult for the case's defenders to continue supporting the Court's decision in light of continued congressional inaction and the repeated failures of the collective bargaining process, both of which had been called on for a solution by all the courts in the Flood litigation. One example of this was "Reconsidering *Flood v. Kuhn*," a 1995 law review article by eminent sports law professor Stephen F. Ross. The article argued that Blackmun's opinion had been "misunderstood" and that "viewed as an example of dynamic and textual statutory interpretation, *Flood* was a justifiable response by a Court concerned that inflexible application of an 1890 statute would ruin a great American institution." Contrary to critics of the decision, Ross argued that *at the time* Justice Blackmun had been both correct and consistent with his own judicial philosophy in accepting baseball's argument that the reserve system was an absolute "necessity" to the preservation of the sport and the competitive balance between the teams and the leagues. However, that was then. Professor Ross's article, written during the disastrous players' strike of 1994–1995, conceded that "after almost two decades of experience with free agency," the chaos and competitive imbalances feared by owners had not materialized. Therefore, since Ross saw "no congressional signals" as of 1995 suggesting that Congress would act to eliminate baseball's exemption, he concluded that "more good than harm" would come if *Flood* was now overruled.

Whatever the reaction to the Court's decision, and the explanations for the outcome, the case by no means ended the quest to do away with the reserve system. It merely shifted the focus back to the collective bargaining process between the players and the owners that had been established with the 1968 Basic Agreement. During the case, this process had been repeatedly cited by both sides in support of their position. The players claimed that judicial intervention was required because the owners had been using the process to avoid dealing with the reserve system, and the owners defended collective bargaining as evidence that judicial involvement was unnecessary. Within three years after *Flood v. Kuhn*, a number of elements related to collective bargaining fell into place that would result in the end of the reserve system as Flood had known it and the rise of free agency. One of those elements came into play during the negotiations that resulted in the 1970 Basic Agreement. Among the new features of that agreement and the bargaining process was the creation of a three-member arbitration panel. The three members of the panel would consist of a players' representative, one from management, and one "impartial arbitrator" agreed to by both sides. The last named was especially important, for now, unless the issue involved the "integrity of the game," the commissioner no longer had the final word on player disputes.

The second element was the reserve system itself. For most of baseball's history up to Flood's lawsuit, common understanding of a player's lifetime obligation to a team centered on that part of the Uniform Players Contract known as the "reserve clause." But as witnesses during Flood's trial (and even earlier during the Celler hearings) had explained, there was no longer a single clause but a number of interconnected provisions; hence the more accurate designation "reserve system." This system had been incorporated into the 1968 Basic Agreement. One of those provisions, Paragraph 10(a), stated that when a player and a club could not agree on terms for the coming year, the club had the "right to renew this contract for a period of one year." The intent seemed clear enough. A player who refused his club's offer and didn't sign his contract would automatically have his current contract renewed (there were stipulations for reductions in salaries) for the upcoming season. That was why Flood had to have Philadelphia trade him to Washington before he could sign with the Senators even though he had never played for the Phillies. In theory, once a player signed that first contract, he could be forced to continue playing for that team for as long as it wanted without ever signing another contract. But was it possible that the "one year" phrase could be interpreted as a *limit* on how long a player could be reserved without having signed his contract, and was this a "loophole" that the players could use to force the reserve issue into arbitration? Miller thought so and had written "that it was only a matter of time, I felt, before we could test whether a club's right of renewal of a contract lasted forever or existed for only one additional year."

The third element that needed to develop was a unified and supportive players' association and players willing and able to bring a grievance before the arbitration panel. Despite Miller's regrets about not doing a better job organizing player support for Flood's legal challenge, under his leadership the MLBPA had become more effective and taken on the characteristics of a true labor union. In the winter of 1968–1969, the players had all refused to sign their contracts until Miller and Kuhn had negotiated changes in Major League Baseball's contributions to the players' pension fund. The following year, they had approved backing Flood's lawsuit, and at the beginning of the 1972 season, Miller and the association had organized a successful players' strike. The strike, again over the pension fund issue, delayed the opening of the regular season and further enhanced the "credibility" of the association in the eyes of the players. Coming just two months before the Supreme Court handed down its ruling in the Flood case, it may explain why the reaction of Kuhn and others on the owners' side to their victory was more circumspect than expected.

The final element to fall into place was players who were eligible to file a grievance under Paragraph 10(a). The Yankees pitcher Al Downing had played the 1969 season without a contract, but at the time, the commissioner, not the new arbitration panel, would have handled his grievance. Prior to the 1972 season, catcher Ted Simmons had rejected the St. Louis Cardinals' contract offer, but when he showed up during spring training, the Cardinals were able to renew his contract and place him on the eligible player list even though he hadn't signed a new contract. What might have been the first test case was ended when he signed a new two-year deal with the club in July. There was speculation that the Cardinals had given him the multiyear contract (and a raise) to avoid the dubious distinction of producing a second test case. In 1973 seven players began the regular season without contracts, but eventually the players either signed during the season (one, Jim Kaat, signed the day before the season began) or were released by their teams.

While waiting for an opportunity to test the arbitration process, the association continued to exert pressure on the owners to modify the reserve system directly. As in the past, the owners refused to consider substantive changes. However, during the negotiations that led to the new Basic Agreement in 1972, the owners did make an interesting concession. The players had proposed that a player, after a certain number of years with the same team, could become a free agent if not offered a certain salary. Instead, it was agreed that veteran players, those with ten years in the same league and five years with the same team, had the right to "veto" a trade to a particular team. In addition, players with two years with the same team could go to salary arbitration, which also explains why the number of potential unsigned players who might test the system dropped in 1974. In Curt Flood's case, since he had been with the Cardinals for twelve years, he would have been able to refuse the trade to Philadelphia. Although he had been offered an increase in salary, he would still have had no choice in what other team he might have played for.

The demise of the reserve system came in 1975. Three players had started the regular season that year without contracts. One, Richie Zisk of Pittsburgh, played the entire season as a renewed player but signed his contract during the postseason playoffs. Andy Messersmith and Dave McNally, pitchers for the Los Angeles Dodgers and Montreal Expos, respectively, both began the season without contracts. Messersmith had refused to sign his when the Dodgers had refused to include a no-trade clause in his contract. At the end of the 1974 season, McNally had been traded to the Expos by Baltimore after an outstanding career with the Orioles (including four consecutive seasons of more than twenty wins). He started the new season without coming to terms with the Expos. But after losing six games in a row, he decided to retire, heading back to his home in Montana, where he ran a car dealership with his brother. Despite attempts by the Expos to lure him back, McNally, who was also a strong supporter of the association, decided to go ahead with the arbitration process and, along with Messersmith, test the one-year provision. In early October 1975 the MLBPA filed grievances on behalf of the two players to be heard by the arbitration panel.

The panel's third "neutral" member was seventy-year-old labor arbitrator Peter Seitz. By this time, Seitz had already dealt with contract-related issues involving players Sparky Lyle and Bobby Tolan. Tolan had played without a contract and was seeking a ruling that would give him free agency. However, during the panel's deliberations, Tolan signed a new contract with his San Diego Padres club. One player to whom Seitz did grant free agency was Oakland pitcher Catfish Hunter, but that case involved a multiyear contract dispute with Athletics owner Chuck Finley and not Paragraph 10(a). As the Messersmith-McNally hearings progressed, Seitz encouraged the owners' lawyer, John Gaherin, and Miller to get the teams to resolve the matter before a final decision. Despite Gaherin's entreaties for the owners to do so, they remained as obstinate as ever in their belief in the sanctity of the reserve system. On December 23, 1975, Seitz ruled in favor of the players. In his ruling he maintained that his role had not been to make any judgment, "good or bad," on the reserve system itself but merely to "interpret and apply the agreements and understanding of the parties." Accordingly, his understanding of Paragraph 10(a) meant that an unsigned player could be reserved for one year and one year only. After that he was a "free agent." So Messersmith and McNally now had the status that Curt Flood had claimed. They were free to negotiate with the team or teams of their choice for the best terms they could arrange. As it happened, McNally returned to Montana and retirement, and Messersmith eventually signed with the Atlanta Braves.

In response to the filing of Messersmith's and McNally's grievances at the beginning of October, the owners returned to the courtroom. They convinced one of their number, Ewing Kauffman of the Kansas City Royals, to file suit on behalf of all the other teams against the MLBPA in federal district court in Kansas City, Missouri. The suit was initiated on October 28, a month before hearings on the players were even held, and challenged the jurisdiction of the arbitration panel to hear the grievances. Since neither side knew the outcome of hearings that hadn't yet been held, it was agreed at a pretrial conference on November 6 that the arbitration panel "should go forward" and that the hearings would "afford the parties a full and fair opportunity to present all arguments based on jurisdictional considerations." Once the panel had made its decision, the owners also challenged the outcome, primarily on the grounds that Seitz, the "impartial arbitrator," had exceeded his authority in awarding free agency to the two players. The owners also suggested that Seitz had not been impartial but rather had imposed "his own philosophy and personal brand of industrial justice." The case was heard before District Court Judge John W. Oliver, a Missouri Democrat appointed to the bench by President Kennedy in 1962. Instead of a regular courtroom trial, Judge Oliver based his final judgment in the case on "formal findings of fact," which the judge accepted or rejected in light of "voluminous" amounts of documentary materials submitted by both sides (including the record of *Flood v. Kuhn*). This material was supplemented by several days of evidentiary hearings of testimony from Major League Baseball officials.

Judge Oliver's decision in *Kansas City Royals Baseball Corporation v. Major League Baseball Players Association* was announced on February 3, 1976. He ruled in favor of the players' association on all claims made by the owners. The arbitration panel did in fact have jurisdiction to hear the grievances and had not exceeded its jurisdiction by formulating "the particular remedy it deemed necessary to enforce its decision." Its award of free agency to Messersmith and McNally should therefore be enforced. Even beyond the favorable ruling for the players this time, Judge Oliver's opinion in the case was remarkably different in some ways from the various rulings in *Flood v. Kuhn*. The biggest difference was the almost complete absence of the kind of excessive deference and nostalgic reverence toward baseball and the owners shown by Judges Cooper, Waterman, and Feinberg and Justice Blackmun. On the contrary, Judge Oliver rejected those findings of "fact and law" related to "the history of how club owners may have run their business in the 19th Century and that portion of the 20th Century before they entered into a collective bargaining agreement" with the players. It was the Basic Agreement of 1968 and its subsequent renewals that determined "the rights of the parties in this case," not the owners' "unilateral" practices prior to that time. Judge Oliver filled his opinion with citations from labor decisions, not lists of great ballplayers or references to our "national pastime" (which may be a reason why the decision is also cited in sports law casebooks).

In his interpretation of the various agreements, Judge Oliver concluded that at no time had the MLBPA ever "acquiesced" in the reserve system, nor had it agreed to any new articles in 1970, and after that the system was excluded as an issue to be resolved by the grievance procedure. Indeed, he expressed his own inability to understand the "distinctions that exist in the Club Owners' minds" when it came to parts of the agreement and their significance to the reserve system. Accordingly, "established principles of federal labor law" required the two parties to submit the players' grievances to the arbitration panel. Once the panel had made its decision, that was the end of it because "applicable federal law" prevented the courts from reviewing "the merits of the grievances submitted to arbitration panels established by collective bargaining agreements" or the opinions of the impartial arbitrators. Although he didn't say so directly, Judge Oliver seemed well aware of the contradictory (hypocritical?) nature of the owners' arguments compared to their position in *Flood v. Kuhn*. Four years earlier, they had urged application of federal "labor policies" and labor laws regarding collective bargaining as controlling and preempting the antitrust issue. Now, having accepted those policies and laws by agreeing to collective bargaining, the club owners wanted the courts to treat baseball as they had before collective bargaining. Judge Oliver would have none of that. Baseball's owners had made their new playing field, and now they would have to play on it.

A month later, on March 9, 1976, a three-judge panel of the Court of Appeals for the Eighth Circuit in Kansas City affirmed Judge Oliver's decision. The court concurred with all of the findings of "fact and law" of the district court and, like the lower court, expressed "no views" on the merits of the reserve system. However, Judges Gerald Heany and Roy Stephenson argued that the arbitration panel's decision did not necessarily "alter" that system, since there still remained various other provisions in the Basic Agreement that "operate to deter a player from 'playing out his option.'" Both club owners and the players' association had agreed on the need for "some form" of reserve system to protect the game's "integrity" and maintain public confidence. Their disagreement came from determining the "degree of control necessary" for both sides to be satisfied. The third member of the panel, Chief Judge John R. Gibson, filed a short concurring opinion. He believed that this case was "closer than perceived" by either Judge Oliver or his fellow appeals court judges. Gibson questioned whether or not there had been a "mutual" understanding in the various versions of the Basic Agreement of "an intent to exclude" matters such as the Messersmith and McNally grievances from the arbitration process. He cautioned against what he called this "presumption of arbitrability" but ultimately agreed that without further evidence, the owners were "stuck with" that presumption.

It would be easy to claim that the Seitz decision and the court rulings upholding his decision marked not only the "demise" of the reserve system and the birth of free agency but also a new era of peace and harmony between baseball club owners and players. Such results would certainly have made a more satisfying ending to the story of Curt Flood's lawsuit. But the story of baseball, the players, and the law most certainly didn't end in 1976. It may have been, to paraphrase Charles Korr and Paul Richards, the end of baseball as they had known it, but over the next three decades, baseball changed in many ways, and the conflicts and struggles between players and owners continued. The main differences were the form and venue of such conflicts. Substantive changes and modifications to what was now referred to as the "free agent system" did come about, as predicted, through the collective bargaining process. But the enhanced solidarity and credibility of the MLBPA, especially under Miller's and then his successor Donald Fehr's leadership, resulted in more traditional forms of collective union actions to secure changes, such as strikes or, in the case of the club owners and Major League commissioner, player "lockouts." The players' pension fund was the issue behind the first players' strike in 1972 and the owners' lockout of the players during spring training in 1973. Between the Seitz decision and 2002, there were six work stoppages, including lockouts in 1976 and 1990 and player strikes in 1980, 1981, 1985, and 1994–1995. All took place before or during negotiations over a new agreement between the association and Major League Baseball, and all involved in some fashion free agency, free-agent compensation, salary arbitration, and salary caps. The 1994 strike was by far the longest and bitterest, lasting 232 days and causing the cancellation of postseason games, including the World Series.

Yet as Leonard Koppett had pointed out back in 1972, player-management relations were only a piece of a much larger picture of the issues and changes that would affect baseball in the years to come. From the players' perspective, Curt Flood's case was all about the reserve system and its stranglehold on ballplayers' freedom and their relationship with the owners of the teams for whom they played. But for the owners, the antitrust issue encompassed other issues that in the long run were just as vital to the well-being of their businesses. These included such things as league expansion and the awarding and switching of franchises, broadcast revenues and rights, and the construction of new stadiums and replacement of older ones. Koppett predicted that the "battleground" for these issues in the future would be Congress, not the courts. And given the owners' huge financial resources and their ability to marshal and use the lobbyists "working in the world of practical politics," the owners would continue to get their way despite the labor issues. Koppett noted that even as he was writing, there were two U.S. Senate committees and one House committee considering legislation aimed at federal regulation of professional sports, including baseball. Nothing came of these bills, and until 1994 the policy of "positive inaction" that Justice Blackmun had talked about in the Flood case continued in Congress.

But the possibility and then the reality of the players' strike starting in August 1994 generated new demands by the public for some sort of congressional response. The strike involved the issues of free agency, minimum salaries, salary arbitration, and revenue sharing. Because it touched so directly on issues of money and escalating player salaries and owner profits, the strike generated a widespread, passionate public outcry against "greedy and overpaid" players and even greedier owners. Even then president Bill Clinton publicly urged a quick settlement on behalf of "little kids . . . and not-so-little kids" who he said wanted to see the season completed. During the fall of 1994, which for the first time since 1905 did not have a World Series, public outrage grew stronger. Finally, in January a bill was introduced in the Senate aimed at eliminating baseball's antitrust exemption. The legislation never made it out of the Judiciary Committee, largely because by that spring a federal judge had forced the reopening of negotiations between the association and the owners by requiring that the 1995 season be played under the expired collective bargaining agreement. The strike finally ended a month into the 1995 season.

Then, on January 21, 1997, the day after Curt Flood died of throat cancer and pneumonia in a Los Angeles hospital, Senator Orrin Hatch of Utah reintroduced the earlier bill. Now titled the Curt Flood Act of 1997, the measure was cosponsored by Senators Patrick Leahy, Strom Thurmond, and Daniel Moynihan. Its proposed purpose was to "clarify that major league baseball players and owners have the same legal rights, and the same restrictions, under the antitrust laws as the players and owners in other professional sports leagues." That summer the Judiciary Committee (which included all four sponsors) held hearings on the bill, with a new lineup of witnesses. Donald Fehr had replaced Marvin Miller as executive director of the MLBPA when Miller had finally stepped down in 1984. Fehr was an attorney who had successfully represented the union in the litigation over the Seitz decision. Bowie Kuhn was also not around, having been ousted by the owners in 1981 (though he served out his term until 1984). Kuhn's successors tended to be short-lived — literally in the case of Bart Giamatti, who had died suddenly in 1989 just 154 days into his term. Appearing before the Judiciary Committee hearings was Allan "Bud" Selig. Although he would become (and is currently) commissioner, at the time he held the position of chairman of the Major League Executive Council (he was president of the Milwaukee Brewers). Stanley M.

Brand, the National League's vice president, also testified on behalf of the owners. Selig and Brand's main concern was convincing Congress to at least maintain baseball's antitrust exemption for the minor leagues, given the "unique relationship" of the minors for the "professional development" of future major leaguers.

In October the bill was voted out of committee on a bipartisan vote, but it was not approved by the entire Congress until the end of January; hence it became the Curt Flood Act of 1998.

The act stated that Major League Baseball players were now covered under the antitrust laws "to the same extent such conduct, acts, practices, or agreements would be subject to the antitrust laws if engaged in by persons in any other professional sports business affecting interstate commerce." Almost the entire act, however, consisted of all those activities and practices *not* subject to the antitrust laws. It was a lengthy list that included everything, and more, that Leonard Koppett had predicted back in 1972 would never be accepted by owners. Everything from "franchise expansion, location or relocation" and "franchise ownership . . . and ownership transfers" to the "marketing and sales of the entertainment product" remained free from antitrust laws. The act also continued to protect from government interference "the relationship between the Office of the Commissioner and franchise owners." The testimony of Selig and Brand had also succeeded in getting an amendment to the final measure, which exempted baseball's minor leagues and their players from the provisions of the act.

It is worth noting that it was the exemption of these aspects of the sport that had concerned those senators on the Judiciary Committee (mostly Democrats) who felt strongly that the act was far too limited in scope. They voted against the bill and in their "Minority Report" argued that all aspects of baseball's operations needed to be placed under federal regulation, as was the case with other professional sports. Moreover, the original House version of the bill excluded only the minor leagues from antitrust laws. Submitted by John Conyers of Michigan, the bill was titled the Baseball Fans and Communities Protection Act of 1997 and was intended to remove baseball's antitrust protection in all aspects of its operation, particularly Major League Baseball's authority over the awarding and location of club franchises. This concern was a response to several recent federal and state cases in which the courts could not agree on whether or not baseball's antitrust exemption could be used either by the league or a state to block an attempt by a club owner to move or sell a club.

On October 28, 1998, President Clinton signed the Curt Flood Act into law. In his signing statement the president noted, "It is especially fitting that this legislation honors a courageous baseball player and individual, the late Curt Flood, whose enormous talents on the baseball diamond were matched by his courage off the field. It was 29 years ago this month that Curt Flood refused a trade from the St. Louis Cardinals to the Philadelphia Phillies. His bold stand set in motion the events that culminate in the bill I have signed into law."

One Man Out

And what about Curt Flood himself? At the time of the Supreme
Court's ruling, Flood had already begun his "self-imposed exile" in
Europe. It was actually his second exile because he had left the States
after his trial before returning to play for the Senators early in the 1971
season. He eventually moved to the Mediterranean island of Majorca,
off the coast of Spain. There he ran a seaside bar called the Rustic Inn
and became "the forgotten man" who "seems to be hiding from the
world." One person who did maintain a connection with Flood during this time was Howard Cosell, the sports commentator who had
been one of the first to interview Curt after the lawsuit had begun, an
interview in which Flood had described himself as a "well-paid slave."
Cosell even managed to track Flood down in Majorca and described
a moving conversation with him that ended with Flood having "tears
in his eyes. In spite of himself he still missed baseball." After bounc-
ing around from Andorra to Puerto Rico to the Dominican Repub-
lic, Flood finally returned to the States in the fall of 1975, settling in
his hometown of Oakland.

According to his biographer Alex Belth, Flood came back to Oakland "a shattered man." Aside from the few writers who wanted to do
a "whatever happened to?" story about him, he was for the most part
ignored, and he seemed to want it that way. He told author Richard
Reeves that he "didn't want to bring it all up again. . . . Do you know
what it's like to be called the little black son of a bitch who tried to
destroy baseball, the American Pastime?" For a short time Flood did
find work as a commentator on television broadcasts of Oakland Athletics games, thanks to his old friend Sam Bercovich and A's owner
Charles Finley (who probably saw hiring Flood as a way to irritate
Bowie Kuhn, whom Finley hated). But Flood was clearly not able to
banter about the game he loved so much in the way commentators are

supposed to talk. He also worked for a time with the Oakland Department of Parks and Aquatics as the "commissioner" of its youth baseball program. It was during these years that Curt faced another personal demon. In 1986 Howard Cosell wrote an article that described the achievements of the man he described as "noble" but also his need for help. Flood had become an alcoholic. The drinking in earnest had begun in Spain but had gotten worse after Flood's return to Oakland. At one point he had fractured his skull falling down some stairs after drinking "a couple of beers too many." Cosell wrote, "Flood has long been finished with baseball, but in truth baseball has not been finished with him," and he pleaded for baseball to give Flood the help that he not only needed but deserved.

By the 1980s things did begin to change in Curt Flood's life. In 1986 he married the actress Judy Pace. They had dated in the years just before his lawsuit and then reconnected in 1985. Like Marion Jorgensen, Pace provided Flood with a measure of stability and support, and he overcame his alcoholism. Just as significantly, Flood slowly began to get the recognition he had been denied. By the 1980s it had become reasonably clear that the owners' dire predictions of chaos and the demise of baseball if the reserve system were eliminated, or even changed, were wrong. Baseball with free agency was doing well, and the players' association was becoming stronger than ever. Now when Flood showed up before games at San Francisco's Candlestick Park or the Oakland Coliseum, players would go up to him and thank him and even ask for advice on their playing. Marvin Miller made a point of reminding players at the start of spring training season that they could thank Curt Flood for their higher salaries. During the players' strike in 1982, Flood was asked whether he regretted what he had done and if he harbored any bitterness toward players who were earning salaries he could not have imagined. His response was to downplay the money part and "think of the dignity players have knowing that their contracts have a date to start and a date to end." For Flood, the important issue in the strike was union solidarity. During the 1980s Flood returned to professional baseball of a sort when he was hired as commissioner of the United Baseball League, an ill-fated attempt to create a veteran ballplayers' league.

In November 1993 the political commentator and baseball fan George F. Will wrote a column about Flood, which he titled "Dred

Scott in Spikes." The immediate purpose of the article was to commemorate an unusual event that had taken place a week earlier. At the annual Golden Gloves Award ceremony, Curt Flood had finally been given the award he had earned for his outstanding outfield play during the 1969 season but had never actually received because of the lawsuit. For Will, the ceremony honored only part of Flood's real legacy for baseball. He described Flood's case: how it had benefited many of the very players who had chosen not to publicly support him and how it had proved wrong the dire consequences predicted by the owners if players had their "freedom." In 1857 the Supreme Court had ruled that Dred Scott, like all other African Americans then, was not a citizen. For Will, "few have ever matched the grace and craftsmanship Curt Flood brought to it [baseball] as a player. However, none matched what he did for the game as a citizen." The following year Curt Flood was featured in episodes of filmmaker Ken Burns's monumental television series *Baseball* as well as in one of the chapters of the companion volume to that series. Several other documentaries about Flood would appear, including one by director Spike Lee; another would be made and widely shown by the ESPN sports cable network.

As time passed and he began to receive more recognition for what he had done, Flood became more philosophical about what he had gone through and what he had accomplished. In one of his last interviews, with *San Francisco Chronicle* reporter Joan Ryan, he admitted:

> I lost money, coaching jobs, a shot at the Hall of Fame. But when you weigh that against all the things that are really and truly important, things that are deep inside you, then I think I've succeeded. People try to make a Greek tragedy of my life and they can't do it. I'm too happy. Remember when I told you about the American dream? That if you worked hard enough, and tried hard enough, and kicked yourself in the butt, you'd succeed. Well, I think I did, I think I did.

It is sometimes the case that heroes are not truly recognized until after they're no longer around, and sadly, that was true for Curt Flood. Flood died of pneumonia in a Los Angeles hospital on January 20, 1997, just two days after his fifty-ninth birthday. He had been diagnosed the previous spring with throat cancer. Interviewed on radio the day after his passing, Public Broadcasting Service sports commentator John Feinstein correctly predicted that "what will happen now is — now that he's dead people will start to notice what a hero he was." Indeed, obituaries around the country praised him as the outfielder "who defied baseball" and as the star center fielder "whose battle led to the free-agent era." Players' association representatives David Cone and Tom Glavine expressed a similar view in their joint statement: "Every major league baseball player owes Curt Flood a debt of gratitude that can never be repaid. With the odds overwhelmingly against him, he was willing to take a stand for what he knew was right."

That was just the beginning. As discussed in Chapter 8, the next year Congress honored Flood by naming the legislation finally removing baseball's antitrust exemption the Curt Flood Act. The same year, his widow, Judy Pace, accepted Flood's posthumous selection to the Baseball Reliquary, a sort of anti–Hall of Fame set up by a California publisher to honor baseball players not simply for their on-field statistics but for their character as well. Another inductee that day was Bill Veeck, one of the few owners who had supported Flood. In her moving acceptance speech on behalf of her husband, Pace proudly pointed out that Curt had also recently been named by *Time* magazine's Daniel Ockrent as one of the ten most influential sports figures of the twentieth century. The one honor denied Flood that might have given him the validation and recognition he desired was selection to the Baseball Hall of Fame in Cooperstown, New York. The hall enshrines players for their outstanding play, and Curt Flood had seemed to be heading toward it at the time he left baseball. However, the Hall of Fame created the Veterans Committee, a sort of "second chance" process in which every two years baseball writers and members of the hall vote from a list of players, managers, umpires, and others who played for at least ten seasons and have been out of the game for at least twenty-one years. In 2003 Flood's name appeared on the veterans' ballot, but he received only 12.5 percent of the vote, far short of the 75 percent needed for election to the Hall of Fame. It was enough to get him on the list two years later, when he again got 12.5 percent of the vote. However, in 2007 his vote was 17.1 percent, guaranteeing him a spot on the 2009 ballot and the possibility of a future plaque in the hall.

Along with his list of baseball greats in *Flood v. Kuhn*, Justice Blackmun wrote of the kind of immortality conferred on the game and its participants by literature. He listed examples of famous baseball works such as the poem "Casey at the Bat." What Blackmun couldn't have known was that the player whose fate he decided would one day achieve that same literary immortality. In 1991 Tim Peeler published a collection of baseball poetry. His "lead-off" poem was titled "Curt Flood," and it might have moved even Justice Blackmun:

> try to tell 'em Curt,
> how you crowned their wallets,
> climbed courtroom steps
> for them
> swallowed that black ball,
> a scapegoat out to pasture.
> they don't remember
> the trash you are
> your greedy headlines,
> the slope of your career.
> you are a ghost at barterer's wing,
> your smoky grey eyes
> are two extra zeroes
> on every contract.

CHRONOLOGY

1869	Harry Wright puts together the first professional baseball team, the Cincinnati Red Stockings.
1876	The National League comes into existence.
1885	The National Brotherhood of Professional Baseball Players is formed.
1890	January: The New York Supreme Court rules in *Metropolitan Exhibition Company v. Ward* that the reserve clause is not enforceable. July: Congress passes the Sherman Antitrust Act.
1900	A Pennsylvania court rules that ballplayer Nap Lajoie's services are unique and irreplaceable.
1903	The National League and American League sign a National Agreement merging leagues and creating a commission to run Major League Baseball. The reserve system is made a part of the agreement, and the reserve clause becomes part of the Uniform Players Contract.
1920	Andrew "Rube" Foster organizes the Negro National League.
1921	The Major Leagues hire Judge Kenesaw Mountain Landis as commissioner to clean up baseball in the wake of the 1919 "Black Sox" scandal.
1922	The U.S. Supreme Court in *Federal Baseball Club v. National League* rules that professional baseball is exempt from federal antitrust laws.
1938	Curtis Charles Flood is born in Houston, Texas.
1946	Danny Gardella challenges the reserve system by playing in Mexico. A federal circuit court upholds *Federal Baseball* but orders a trial. Gardella drops the suit before the trial begins.
1947	Jackie Robinson breaks baseball's "color barrier" as the first African American to play in the Major Leagues.
1951	The Celler Committee begins the first of many congressional hearings over the next three decades to consider legislation regulating baseball and removing its antitrust exemption.
1953	The U.S. Supreme Court reaffirms baseball's antitrust exemption in the *Toolson* case.
1955	Flood signs his first Major League contract with the Cincinnati Reds and plays in his first game on September 9.

1957	At the end of the 1957 season, Flood is traded to the St. Louis Cardinals.
1963	Flood earns the first of his six consecutive Gold Gloves for outstanding fielding.
1964	Flood is selected to the National League's all-star team for the first time, and the Cardinals win the World Series against the New York Yankees.
1966	The Major League Baseball Players Association (MLBPA) hires Marvin Miller as its full-time executive director.
1967	Flood sets the record for consecutive games without an error. The Cardinals win their second World Series in three years against the Boston Red Sox.
1968	The first Basic Agreement is signed between baseball owners and the MLBPA.
1969	In October, Flood is notified that he is being traded to Philadelphia Phillies.
1970	January 16: Flood files suit in New York District Court. May 19: The trial begins in federal district court in Manhattan. May 21: A new Basic Agreement is reached between owners and the MLBPA. June 9: The trial in the Flood case ends. August 12: Judge Cooper hands down a decision against Flood. August 24: An appeal is filed in the Circuit Court of Appeals in New York. November 3: Flood signs with the Washington Senators.
1971	January 24: Arguments are held before the Court of Appeals. April 7: The Court of Appeals upholds the district court ruling. April 27: Flood leaves the Senators and flies to Europe. October 19: The U.S. Supreme Court agrees to hear *Flood v. Kuhn*.
1972	March 20: Oral arguments are held before the Supreme Court. June 19: The Supreme Court announces a decision in *Flood v. Kuhn*, once more reaffirming the 1922 *Federal Baseball* ruling.
1975	The arbitration panel's Peter Seitz rules that Andy Messersmith and Dave McNally are free agents.
1997	Curt Flood dies in Los Angeles after battling throat cancer.
1998	Congress passes the Curt Flood Act, repealing baseball's antitrust exemption.

RELEVANT CASES

American League Baseball Club of Chicago v. Harold H. Chase, 149 N.Y. Supp. 6 (1914)

Federal Baseball Club v. National League of Professional Baseball, et al., 259 U.S. 200 (1922)

Flood v. Kuhn, 70 Civ. 202 (1970), 443 F. 2nd 264 (1971) affirmed, 407 U.S. 258 (1972)

Gardella v. Chandler, 172 F. 2nd 402 (2nd Cir. 1949)

Kansas City Royals Baseball Corporation v. Major League Players Association, 409 F. Supp. 233 (1976), appeal 532 F. 2nd 615 (1976)

Lumley v. Wagner, 42 Eng. Rep. 687 (1852) *Metropolitan Exhibition Company v. Ewing*, 42 N.E.198 (S.D.N.Y. 1890)

Metropolitan Exhibition Co. v. Ward, 9 NYS 779 (N.Y. Sup. Ct. 1890)

Philadelphia Ball Club Ltd. v. Lajoie, 202 Pa 210, 51 A 973 (1902)

Radovich v. National Football League, 352 U.S. 445 (1957)

Salerno v. American League, 429 F. 2d 1003 (2nd Cir. 1970), cert. denied

Salerno v. Kuhn, 400 U.S. 1001 (1971)

Toolson v. New York Yankees, 346 U.S. 356 (1953)

U.S. v. E. C. Knight Co., 156 U.S. 1 (1895)

BIBLIOGRAPHICAL ESSAY

Note from the Series Editors: The following bibliographical essay contains the primary and secondary sources the author consulted for this volume. We have asked all authors in the series to omit formal citations in order to make our volumes more readable, inexpensive, and appealing for students and general readers.

The most important primary sources for this study were the Supreme Court Case Files, No. 71-32, *Flood v. Kuhn*, at the National Archives (Washington, D.C.), and the United States Supreme Court Records and Briefs, vol. 407, in the Library of Congress (Washington, D.C.). The records of the district court trial can be found in Record Group 21, Records of District Courts of the United States, 1865–1991, National Archives, Northeast Region (New York City). The various court opinions discussed can be found by citation in the Federal Reports and the various official state court reports as cited. The notes on the Supreme Court's conference and initial vote in the case can be found in Del Dickson, *The Supreme Court in Conference (1940–1985)* (New York: Oxford University Press, 2001). The Celler Committee hearings on baseball in the 1950s are based on "Hearings before the Anti-trust Subcommittee, Committee on the Judiciary," House of Representatives, 82nd Congress, 1st Session, Parts 1, 2, and 3, Serial No. 8 (Washington, D.C.: Government Printing Office); and "Organized Baseball": Report of the Subcommittee on Study of Monopoly Power of the Committee on the Judiciary, U.S. Senate, 83rd Congress, 2nd Session, 1954. See also the Curt Flood Act of 1997, U.S. Senate, 105th Congress, 1st Session. The press coverage of Flood's career and lawsuit was extensive, and many of these articles have been collected in the holdings of the Baseball Hall of Fame library in Cooperstown, New York. Particularly useful for the Supreme Court are the recently opened Harry Blackmun Papers in the Manuscript Division of the Library of Congress, which include Blackmun's handwritten notes on the case. In addition, The Justice Harry A. Blackmun Oral History Project in the Library of Congress includes interviews in which the justice talks about the case. The library's Manuscript Division also contains the Arthur Goldberg Papers, which have some material relating to the case.

There are also a number of useful edited collections of documentary material related to the history of baseball and legal issues: Spencer W. Waller, Neil B. Cohen, and Paul Finkelman, eds., *Baseball and the American Legal Mind* (New York: Garland, 1995); Dean A. Sullivan, ed., *Middle Innings: A Documentary History of Baseball, 1900–1948* (Lincoln: University of Nebraska Press, 2001); and Dean A. Sullivan, ed., *Late Innings: A Documentary History of Baseball, 1945–1972* (Lincoln: University of Nebraska Press, 2002). Documents relating to the business and history of baseball can also be found on the web-sites of the Society of American Baseball Research (SABR), Major League Baseball, and the Major League Baseball Players Association. Personal memoirs and autobiographies are not normally thought of or available as a source in the writing of sports history. Flood's case is a welcome exception insofar as there are a number of such works, most notably Curt Flood's memoir *The Way It Is* (New York: Trident Press, 1971). Also relevant are Marvin Miller, *A Whole Different Ball Game: The Inside Story of the Baseball Revolution* (Chicago: Ivan R. Dee, 2004); Bowie Kuhn, *Hardball: The Education of a Baseball Commissioner* (Lincoln: University of Nebraska Press, 1997); Jackie Robinson, *I Never Had It Made: An Autobiography* (Hopewell, NJ: Ecco Press, 1995); Bill Veeck, *Veeck—as in Wreck: The Autobiography of Bill Veeck* (Chicago: University of Chicago Press, 2001); Albert G. Spaulding, *America's National Game* (San Francisco: Halo Books, 1991); and Red Schoendienst, *Red: A Baseball Life* (Champaign, IL: Sports Publishing, 1995).

There are innumerable histories that cover baseball in its entirety as well as specific periods or aspects of the game. Some of the general ones are Geoffrey C. Ward and Ken Burns, *Baseball: An Illustrated History* (New York: Knopf, 1994); Leonard Koppett, *Koppett's Concise History of Major League Baseball*, expanded ed. (New York: Carroll and Graff, 2004); John Helyar, *Lords of the Realm: The Real History of Baseball* (New York: Ballantine, 1994); Benjamin G. Rader, *Baseball: A History of America's Game* (Urbana: University of Illinois Press, 2002); Donald Dewey and Nicolas Acocella, *The New Biographical History of Baseball* (Chicago: Triumph Books, 2004); and Joseph Wallace, *The Autobiography of Baseball* (New York: Harry N. Abrams, 1998). Statistical information on baseball can be found in John Thorn, Peter Palmer, Michael Gershman, and David Pietrusza, *Total Baseball*, 6th ed. (New York: Total Sports, 1999); Burt Solomon, *The Baseball Timeline* (New York: DK Publishers, 2001); and Society for American Baseball Research, *The SABR Baseball List and Record Book* (New York: Scribner, 2007). The early period of professional baseball, including the origins of the reserve clause, is covered in Harold Seymour, *Baseball: The Early Years* (New York: Oxford University Press, 1989). Also relevant is Peter Levine, *A. G. Spaulding and the Rise of Baseball* (New York: Oxford University Press, 1985). An entertaining version of the ancient origins of baseball is David Block, *Baseball before We Knew It* (Lincoln: University of Nebraska Press, 2005). An interesting comparative study of baseball and soccer is Stephan Szymanski and Andrew Zimbalist, *National Pastime: How Americans Play Baseball and the Rest of the World Plays Soccer* (Washington, D.C.: Brookings Institution Press, 2005). Some of the extensive and growing body of studies that deal with the history of African Americans and baseball are Robert Peterson, *Only the Ball Was White* (New York: Oxford University Press, 1970); Neil Lanctot, *Negro League Baseball: The Rise and Ruin of a Black Insti-*

tution (Philadelphia: University of Pennsylvania Press, 2004); Lawrence D. Hogan, *Shades of Glory: The Negro Leagues and the Story of African-American Baseball* (Cooperstown, NY: National Baseball Hall of Fame and Museum, 2006); Carl Fussman, *After Jackie: Pride, Prejudice, and Baseball's Forgotten Heroes: An Oral History* (New York: ESPN Books, 2007); Bruce Adelson, *Brushing Back Jim Crow: The Integration of Minor League Baseball in the American South* (Charlottesville: University Press of Virginia, 1999); Howard Bryant, *Shut Out: A Story of Race and Baseball in Boston* (New York: Routledge, 2002); Jules Tygiel, *Extra Bases: Reflections on Jackie Robinson, Race, and Baseball History* (Lincoln: University of Nebraska Press, 2002); Robert Elias, ed., *Baseball and the American Dream: Race, Class, Gender and the National Pastime* (New York: M. E. Sharpe, 2001); and William C. Rhoden, *Forty Million Dollar Slaves: The Rise, Fall and Redemption of the Black Athlete* (New York: Crown Publishers, 2006). The current state of African Americans in baseball is covered in Hall of Fame outfielder Dave Winfield's *Dropping the Ball: Baseball's Troubles and How We Can and Must Solve Them* (New York: Scribner, 2007). The story of the St. Louis Cardinals can be found in Peter Golenbock, *The Spirit of St. Louis: A History of the St. Louis Cardinals and Browns* (New York: HarperCollins, 2000); and Roger D. Launius, *Seasons in the Sun: The Story of Big League Baseball in Missouri* (Columbia: University of Missouri Press, 2002).

Two excellent studies on the evolution of baseball and antitrust law are Jerold J. Duquette, *Regulating the National Pastime: Baseball and Antitrust* (Westport, CT: Praeger, 1999); and Roger I. Abrams, *Legal Bases: Baseball and the Law* (Philadelphia: Temple University Press, 1998). For the connections between law and baseball, see Paul Finkelman, "Baseball and the Rule of Law," *Cleveland State Law Review* 46, no. 2 (1998): 239–259. The story of the relationship between owners and players is exhaustively covered in Robert F. Burk, *Never Just a Game: Players, Owners, and American Baseball to 1920* (Chapel Hill: University of North Carolina Press, 1994); and Robert F. Burk, *Much More than a Game: Players, Owners, and American Baseball since 1921* (Chapel Hill: University of North Carolina Press, 2001). The definitive history of the Major League Baseball Players Association is Charles P. Korr, *The End of Baseball as We Knew It: The Players Union, 1960–81* (Champaign: University of Illinois Press, 2002). The best account of baseball's transformation into our "national pastime" is G. Edward White, *Creating the National Pastime: Baseball Transforms Itself, 1903–1953* (Princeton, NJ: Princeton University Press, 1996). See also David Mandell, "Danny Gardella and the Reserve Clause," in *National Pastime: A Review of Baseball History*, no. 26 (2006): 41–44; and Stew Thornley, "The Demise of the Reserve Clause: The Players' Path to Freedom," *National Pastime: A Review of Baseball History*, no. 35 (2007): 115–123.

The general constitutional and legal history background are covered in

Michael Les Benedict, *The Blessings of Liberty: A Concise History of the Constitution of the United States* (Boston: Houghton Mifflin, 2006); Melvin I. Urofsky and Paul Finkelman, *A March of Liberty: A Constitutional History of the United States* (New York: Oxford University Press, 2004); Lawrence M. Friedman, *A History of American Law* (New York: Simon & Schuster, 1973); Lawrence M. Friedman, *American Law in the 20th Century* (New Haven, CT: Yale University Press, 2005); and Bernard Schwartz, *A History of the Supreme Court* (New York: Oxford University Press, 1993). The origins and background of the Sherman Act can be found in William Letwin, *Law and Economic Policy in America: The Evolution of the Sherman Antitrust Act* (Chicago: University of Chicago Press, 1965). Popular, and largely critical, works that focus on the Supreme Court during the tenure of Chief Justice Burger include Bob Woodward and Scott Armstrong, *The Brethren: Inside the Supreme Court* (New York: Avon Books, 1981); and James F. Simon, *In His Own Image: The Supreme Court in Richard Nixon's America* (New York: David McKay, 1973). More scholarly but no less critical are Bernard Schwartz, *The New Right and the Constitution: Turning Back the Legal Clock* (Boston: Northeastern University Press, 1990); and Vincent Blasi, ed., *The Burger Court: The Counter-revolution That Wasn't* (New Haven, CT: Yale University Press, 1983). Information about the justices on the Court can be found in Melvin I. Urofsky, ed., *The Supreme Court Justices: A Biographical Dictionary* (New York: Garland, 1994); and the older but still useful essays in Leon Friedman, *The Justices of the United States Supreme Court, 1789–1978: Their Lives and Major Opinions*, 5 vols. (New York: Chelsea House, 1980). More detailed biographical studies of the justices include G. Edward White, *Justice Oliver Wendell Holmes: Law and the Inner Self* (New York: Oxford University Press, 1993); Stephan L. Wasby, ed., *"He Shall Not Pass This Way Again": The Legacy of Justice William O. Douglas* (Pittsburgh, PA: University of Pittsburgh Press, 1990); Mark Tushnet, *Making Constitutional Law: Thurgood Marshall and the Supreme Court, 1961–1991* (New York: Oxford University Press, 1997); and John C. Jeffries, *Justice Lewis C. Powell* (New York: Fordham University Press, 2001). Surprisingly, the most recent biography of Justice Blackmun does not discuss his "favorite" case: Linda Greenhouse, *Becoming Justice Blackmun: Harry Blackmun's Supreme Court Journey* (New York: Times Books, 2005).

Although there have been many articles and sections of books devoted to Curt Flood and his case, it is only recently that there have been book-length studies: Alex Belth, *Stepping Up: The Story of Curt Flood and His Fight for Baseball Players' Rights* (New York: Persea Books, 2006); Brad Snyder, *A Well-Paid Slave* (New York: Viking, 2006); and Stuart L. Weiss, *The Curt Flood Story: The Man behind the Myth* (Columbia: University of Missouri Press, 2007). All three are well-researched and detailed accounts of Flood's life and career. The Belth and Snyder books are clearly sympathetic to Flood; the Weiss biography is much less so. See also George F. Will, "Dred Scott in Spikes," *Bunts: Curt Flood, Camden Yards, Pete Rose and Other Reflections on Baseball* (New York: Scribner, 1999). Gregg Ivers, "Before Free Agency: How Curt Flood Changed Major League Baseball" (unpublished manuscript, George Washington University, Washington, D.C., 2002), analyzes the case in terms of interest-group dynamics.

The evolution and legal impact of the Curt Flood Act of 1998 have also been richly explored. See Stephen D. Guschow, "The Exemption of Baseball from Federal Anti-trust Laws: A Legal History," *Baseball Research Journal*, no. 23 (1994): 69–70; and Edmund P. Edmonds and William H. Manz, eds., *Baseball and Antitrust: The Legislative History of the Curt Flood Act of 1998, Public Law No. 105-297, 112 Stat. 2824* (Buffalo, NY: William S. Hein & Co., 2001). The spring 1999 issue of Marquette University's *Sports Law Journal* was devoted to a "Symposium: The Curt Flood Act": See *Marquette Sports Law Journal* 9, no. 2 (1999): 306–444. See also Lacie L. Kaiser, "Revisiting the Impact of the Curt Flood Act of 1998 on the Bargaining Relationship between Players and Management in Major League Baseball," *DePaul Law Review* 96 (Fall 2004): 230–263.

Finally, there are a number of works about baseball that do not fit into any of these categories. The poem "Curt Flood" is from Tim Peeler, *Touching All the Bases: Poems from Baseball* (Jefferson, NC: McFarland & Co., 2000). Flood also makes a literary appearance in author Philip Roth's political satire of the Nixon administration, *Our Gang: Starring Tricky and His Friends* (New York: Random House, 1971). The title of this book is a variation on Eliot Asinof's well-known book on the 1919 Black Sox scandal, *Eight Men Out: The Black Sox and the 1919 World Series* (New York: Ace Publishing, 1963). Of course I have no intention of comparing Curt Flood and what he did with the actions of those earlier players. The "convergences" of baseball and law are examined from a unique perspective in several of the essays in Eric Bronson, ed., *Baseball and Philosophy: Thinking outside the Batter's Box* (Chicago: Open Court, 2004).

INDEX